Landscape for a
Good Woman

Landscape for a Good Woman

A Story of Two Lives

Carolyn Kay Steedman

 Rutgers University Press
New Brunswick, New Jersey

Third paperback printing, 1992
Second paperback printing, 1991

First published in the United States by
Rutgers University Press, 1987

First published in Great Britain by
Virago Press Limited, 1986

Library of Congress Cataloging-in-Publication Data
Steedman, Carolyn.
  Landscape for a good woman.

  Bibliography: p.
  Includes index.
  1. Steedman, Carolyn. 2. Sociologists—Great
Britain—Biography. 3. Mothers and daughters—
Great Britain—Case studies. I. Title.
HM22.G8S847 1987   306.8′743   87-4614
ISBN 0-8135-1257-3
ISBN 0-8135-1258-1 (pbk)

I speak now in relation between the Oppressor and the oppressed; the inward bondages I meddle not with in this place, though I am assured that if it be rightly searched into, the inward bondages of minde, as covetousness, pride, hypocrisie, envy, sorrow, fears, desperation and madness, are all occasioned by the outward bondage, that one sort of people lay upon another.

(Gerrard Winstanley, 'The Law of Freedom in a Platform; or, True Magistracy Restored', 1652)

Contents

Acknowledgements

The idea was Carmen Callil's, who saw from reading the Introduction to Kathleen Woodward's *Jipping Street* that there was much more to say. Ursula Owen waited a long time for me to work out what that was. I would like to thank her for her patient and determined editing. Part of the chapter 'The Weaver's Daughter' has appeared in Liz Heron (ed.), *Truth, Dare or Promise: Girls Growing Up in the Fifties*, Virago, 1985. My thanks to Liz Heron for the opportunity to write that piece, and for her many comments and suggestions. Without the practical support of Basil Bernstein and the University of London Institute of Education Sociology Department, this book would not have been written at all. Gill Frith has read and re-read many versions of this: for her my warmest and deepest thanks. I am grateful too to Jane Miller, Terry Lovell, Sally Alexander, Dick Leith and Cora Kaplan for all their good and practical advice (though I have not always taken it). Jenny Richardson helped with the more recent history: thanks and affection.

In the following pages, many references are made to Hans Christian Andersen's two stories 'The Snow Queen' and 'The Little Mermaid'. The edition that I have used here for reference is the Heinemann one of 1900, translated by H. L. Braekstad, in two volumes and with an Introduction by Edmund Gosse. I have no record of the volume I read as a child.

Death of a Good Woman

She died like this. I didn't witness it. My niece told me this. She'd moved everything down into the kitchen: a single bed, the television, the calor-gas heater. She said it was to save fuel. The rest of the house was dark and shrouded. Through the window was only the fence and the kitchen wall of the house next door. Her quilt was sewn into a piece of pink flannelette. Afterwards, there were bags and bags of washing to do. She had cancer, had gone back to Food Reform, talked to me about curing it when I paid my first visit in nine years, two weeks before her death: my last visit. She asked me if I remembered the woman in the health-food shop, when I was about eight or nine, pointing out a man who'd cured cancer by eating watercress. She complained of pains, but wouldn't take the morphine tablets. It was pains everywhere, not in the lungs where the cancer was. It wasn't the cancer that killed: a blood clot travelled from her leg and stopped her heart. Afterwards, the doctor said she'd been out of touch with reality.

We'd known all our childhood that she was a good mother: she'd told us so: we'd never gone hungry; she went out to work for us; we had warm beds to lie in at night. She had conducted a small and ineffective war against the body's fate by eating brown bread, by not drinking, by giving up smoking years ago. To have cancer was the final unfairness in a life measured out by it. She'd been good; it hadn't worked.

Upstairs, a long time ago, she had cried, standing on the bare floorboards in the front bedroom just after we moved to this house in Streatham Hill in 1951, my baby sister in her carry-cot. We both watched the dumpy retreating figure of the health visitor through the curtainless windows. The woman had said: 'This house isn't fit for a baby.' And then she stopped crying, my mother, got by, the phrase that picks up after all difficulty (it says: it's like this; it shouldn't be like this; it's unfair; I'll manage): 'Hard lines, eh, Kay?' (Kay was the name I was called at home, my middle name, one of my father's names).

And I? I will do everything and anything until the end of my days to stop anyone ever talking to me like that woman talked to my mother. It is in this place, this bare, curtainless bedroom that lies my secret and shameful defiance. I read a woman's book, meet such a woman at a party (a woman now, like me) and think quite deliberately as we talk: we are divided: a hundred years ago I'd have been cleaning your shoes. I know this and you don't.

Simone de Beauvoir wrote of her mother's death, said that in spite of the pain it was an easy one: an upper-class death. Outside, for the poor, dying is a different matter:

> And then in the public wards when the last hour is coming near, they put a screen round a dying man's bed: he has seen this screen round other beds that were empty the next day: he knows. I pictured Maman, blinded for hours by the black sun that no one can look at directly: the horror of her staring eyes with their dilated pupils.[1]

Like this: she flung up her left arm over her head, pulled her knees up, looked out with an extraordinary surprise. She lived alone, she died alone: a working-class life, a working-class death.

Part one

Stories

The present tense of the verb *to be* refers only to the present: but nevertheless with the first person singular in front of it, it absorbs the past which is inseparable from it. 'I am' includes all that has made me so. It is more than a statement of immediate fact: it is already biographical.

(John Berger, *About Looking*)[1]

Stories

This book is about lives lived out on the borderlands, lives for which the central interpretative devices of the culture don't quite work. It has a childhood at its centre – my childhood, a personal past – and it is about the disruption of that fifties childhood by the one my mother had lived out before me, and the stories she told about it. Now, the narrative of both these childhoods can be elaborated by the marginal and secret stories that other working-class girls and women from a recent historical past have to tell.

This book, then, is about interpretations, about the places where we rework what has already happened to give current events meaning. It is about the stories we make for ourselves, and the social specificity of our understanding of those stories. The childhood dreams recounted in this book, the fantasies, the particular and remembered events of a South London fifties childhood do not, by themselves, constitute its point. We all return to memories and dreams like this, again and again; the story we tell of our own life is reshaped around them. But the point doesn't lie there, back in the past, back in the lost time at which they happened; the only point lies in interpretation. The past is re-used through the agency of social information, and that interpretation of it can only be made with what people know of a social world and their place within it. It matters then, whether one reshapes past time, re-uses the ordinary exigencies and crises of all childhoods whilst looking down from the curtainless windows of a terraced house like my mother did, or sees at that moment the long view stretching away from the big house in some richer and more detailed landscape.

All children experience a first loss, a first exclusion; lives shape themselves around this sense of being cut off and denied. The health visitor repeated the exclusion in the disdainful language of class, told my mother exactly what it was she stood outside. It is a proposition of this book that that specificity of place and politics has to be reckoned with in making an account of anybody's life, and their use of their own past.

My mother's longing shaped my own childhood. From a Lancashire mill town and a working-class twenties childhood she came away wanting: fine clothes, glamour, money; to be what she wasn't. However that longing was produced in her distant childhood, what she actually wanted were real things, real entities, things she materially lacked, things that a culture and a social system withheld from her. The story she told was about this wanting, and it remained a resolutely social story. When the world didn't deliver the goods, she held the world to blame. In this way, the story she told was a form of political analysis, that allows a political interpretation to be made of her life.

Personal interpretations of past time – the stories that people tell themselves in order to explain how they got to the place they currently inhabit – are often in deep and ambiguous conflict with the official interpretative devices of a culture. This book is organized around a conflict like this, taking as a starting point the structures of class analysis and schools of cultural criticism that cannot deal with everything there is to say about my mother's life. My mother was a single parent for most of her adulthood, who had children, but who also, in a quite particular way, didn't want them. She was a woman who finds no place in the iconography of working-class motherhood that Jeremy Seabrook presents in *Working Class Childhood*, and who is not to be found in Richard Hoggart's landscape. She ran a working-class household far away from the traditional communities of class, in exile and isolation, and in which a man was not a master, nor even there very much. Surrounded as a child by the articulated politics of class-consciousness, she became a working-class Conservative, the only political form that allowed her to reveal the politics of envy.

Many of these ambiguities raise central questions about gender as well as class, and the development of gender in particular social and class circumstances. So the usefulness of the biographical and autobiographical core of the book lies in the challenge it may offer to much of our conventional understanding of childhood, working-class childhood, and little-girlhood. In particular, it challenges the tradition of cultural criticism in this country, which has celebrated a kind of psychological simplicity in the lives lived out in Hoggart's endless streets of little houses. It can help reverse a central question within feminism and psychoanalysis, about the reproduction of the desire to mother in little girls, and replace it with a consideration of women who, by refusing to mother, have refused to reproduce themselves or the circumstances of their exile. The personal past that this book deals with can also serve to raise the question of what happens to theories of patriarchy in households where a father's position is not confirmed by the social world outside the front door. And the story of two lives that follows points finally to a consideration of what people – particularly working-class children of the recent past – come to understand of themselves when all they possess is their labour, and what becomes of the notion of class-consciousness when it is seen as a structure of feeling that can be learned in childhood, with one of its components a proper envy, the desire of people for the things of the earth. Class and gender, and their articulations, are the bits and pieces from which psychological selfhood is made.

*

I grew up in the 1950s, the place and time now located as the first scene of Labour's failure to grasp the political consciousness of its constituency and its eschewal of socialism in favour of welfare philanthropism.[2] But the left had failed

with my mother long before the 1950s. A working-class
Conservative from a traditional Labour background, she
shaped my childhood by the stories she carried from her
own, and from an earlier family history. They were stories
designed to show me the terrible unfairness of things, the
subterranean culture of longing for that which one can
never have. These stories can be used now to show my
mother's dogged search, using what politics came to hand,
for a public form to embody such longing.

Her envy, her sense of the unfairness of things, could not
be directly translated into political understanding, and certainly could not be used by the left to shape an articulated
politics of class. What follows offers no account of that
particular political failure. It is rather an attempt to use that
failure, which has been delineated by historians writing
from quite different perspectives and for quite different
purposes, as a device that may help to explain a particular
childhood, and out of that childhood explain an individual
life lived in historical time. This is not to say that this book
involves a search for a past, or for what really happened.[3] It
is about how people use the past to tell the stories of their
life. So the evidence presented here is of a different order
from the biographical; it is about the experience of my own
childhood, and the way in which my mother re-asserted,
reversed and restructured her own within mine.

Envy as a political motive has always been condemned: a
fierce morality pervades what little writing there is on the
subject. Fiercely moral as well, the tradition of cultural
criticism in this country has, by ignoring feelings like these,
given us the map of an upright and decent country. Out of
this tradition has come Jeremy Seabrook's *Working Class
Childhood* and its nostalgia for a time when people who
were 'united against cruel material privations . . . discovered the possibilities of the human consolations they
could offer each other', and its celebration of the upbringing
that produced the psychic structure of 'the old working
class'.[4] I take a defiant pleasure in the way that my mother's

story can be used to subvert this account. Born into 'the old working class', she wanted: a New Look skirt, a timbered country cottage, to marry a prince.

The very devices that are intended to give expression to childhoods like mine and my mother's actually deny their expression. The problem with most childhoods lived out in households maintained by social class III (manual), IV and V parents is that they simply are not bad enough to be worthy of attention. The literary form that allows presentation of working-class childhood, the working-class autobiography, reveals its mainspring in the title of books like *Born to Struggle; Poverty, Hardship, But Happiness; Growing Up Poor in East London; Coronation Cups and Jam Jars* – and I am deeply aware of the ambiguities that attach to the childhood I am about to recount. Not only was it not very bad, or only bad in a way that working-class autobiography doesn't deal in, but also a particular set of emotional and psychological circumstances ensured that at the time, and for many years after it was over and I had escaped, I thought of it as *ordinary*, a period of relative material ease, just like everybody else's childhood.

I read female working-class autobiography obsessively when I was in my twenties and early thirties (a reading that involved much repetition: it's a small corpus), and whilst I wept over Catherine Cookson's *Our Kate* I felt a simultaneous distance from the Edwardian child who fetched beer bare-footed for an alcoholic mother, the Kate of the title (I have to make it very clear that my childhood was really *not* like that). But it bore a relationship to a personal reality that I did not yet know about: what I now see in the book is its fine delineation of the feeling of being on the outside, outside the law; for Catherine Cookson was illegitimate.[5]

In 1928, when Kathleen Woodward, who had grown up in not-too-bad Peckham, South London, wrote *Jipping Street*, she set her childhood in Bermondsey, in a place of abject and abandoned poverty, 'practically off the map, derelict', and in this manner found a way, within an established literary form, of expressing a complexity of feeling about her personal past that the form itself did not allow.[6]

The tradition of cultural criticism that has employed working-class lives, and their rare expression in literature, had made solid and concrete the absence of psychological individuality – of subjectivity – that Kathleen Woodward struggled against in *Jipping Street*. 'In poor societies,' writes Jeremy Seabrook in *Working Class Childhood*

> where survival is more important than elaboration of relationships, the kind of ferocious personal struggles that lock people together in our own more leisured society are less known.[7]

But by making this distinction, the very testimony to the continuing reverberation of pain and loss, absence and desire in childhood, which is made manifest in the words of 'the old working-class' people that make up much of *Working Class Childhood*, is actually denied.

It would not be possible, in fact, to write a book called 'Middle Class Childhood' (this in spite of the fact that the shelves groan with psychoanalytic, developmental and literary accounts of such childhoods) and get the same kind of response from readers. It's a faintly titillating title, carrying the promise that some kind of pathology is about to be investigated. What is more, in *Working Class Childhood* the discussion of childhood and what our society has done to the idea of childhood becomes the vehicle for an anguished rejection of post-War materialism, the metaphor for all that has gone wrong with the old politics of class and the stance of the labour movement towards the desires that capitalism has inculcated in those who are seen as the passive poor. An analysis like this denies its subjects a particular story, a personal history, except when that story illustrates a general thesis; and it denies the child, and the child who continues to live in the adult it becomes, both an unconscious life, and a particular and developing consciousness of the meanings presented by the social world.

Twenty years before *Working Class Childhood* was written, Richard Hoggart explored a similar passivity of emotional life in working-class communities, what in *The Uses of Literacy* he revealingly called 'Landscape with Figures: A Setting' – a place where in his own memories of the 1920s and 1930s and in his description of similar communities of the 1950s, most people lacked 'any feeling that some change can, or indeed ought to be made in the general pattern of life'.[8] All of Seabrook's corpus deals in the same way with what he sees as 'the falling into decay of a life once believed by those who shared it to be the only admissible form that life could take'.[9] I want to open the door of one of the terraced houses, in a mill town in the 1920s, show Seabrook my mother and her longing, make him see the child of my imagination sitting by an empty grate, reading a tale that tells her a goose-girl can marry a king.

Heaviness of time lies on the pages of *The Uses of Literacy*. The streets are all the same; nothing changes. Writing about the structure of a child's life, Seabrook notes that as recently as thirty years ago (that is, in the 1950s, the time of my own childhood) the week was measured out by each day's function – wash-day, market-day, the day for ironing – and the day itself timed by 'cradling and comforting' ritual.[10] This extraordinary attribution of sameness and the acceptance of sameness to generations of lives arises from several sources. First of all, delineation of emotional and psychological selfhood has been made by and through the testimony of people in a central relationship to the dominant culture, that is to say by and through people who are not working class. This is an obvious point, but it measures out an immensely complicated and contradictory area of historical development that has scarcely yet been investigated. Superficially, it might be said that historians, failing to find evidence of most people's emotional or psycho-sexual existence, have simply assumed that there can't have been much there to find. Such an assumption ignores the structuring of late nineteenth- and early twentieth-century psychology and psychoanalysis, and the way in which the lived experience of the majority of people in a class society has been pathologized and marginalized. When the sons of the working class, who have made their earlier escape from this landscape of psychological simplicity, put so much effort into accepting and celebrating it, into delineating a background of uniformity and passivity, in which pain, loss, love, anxiety and desire are washed over with a patina of stolid emotional sameness, then something important, and odd, and possibly promising of startling revelation, is actually going on. This refusal of a complicated psychology to those living in conditions of material distress is a central theme of this book, and will be considered again in its third section.

The attribution of psychological simplicity to working-class people also derives from the positioning of mental life within Marxism:

> Mental life flows from material conditions. Social being is determined above all by class position – location within the realm of production. Consciousness and politics, all mental conceptions spring from material forces and the relations of production and so reflect these class origins.

This description is Sally Alexander's summary of Marx's 'Preface to a Contribution to the Critique of Political Economy', and of his thesis, expressed here and elsewhere, that 'the mode of production of material life conditions the general process of social, political and mental life'.[11] The attribution of simplicity to the mental life of working people is not, of course, made either in the original, nor in this particular critique of it. But like any theory developed in a social world, the notion of consciousness as located within the realm of production draws on the reality of that world. It is in the 'Preface' itself that Marx mentions his move to

London in the 1850s as offering among other advantages 'a convenient vantage point for the observation of bourgeois society', and which indeed he did observe, and live within, in the novels he and his family read, in family theatricals, in dinner-table talk: a mental life apparently much richer than that of the subjects of his theories. Lacking such possessions of culture, working-class people have come to be seen, within the field of cultural criticism, as bearing the elemental simplicity of class-consciousness and little more.

Technically, class-consciousness has not been conceived of as *psychological* consciousness. It has been separated from 'the empirically given, and from the psychologically describable and explicable ideas that men form about their situation in life', and has been seen rather as a possible set of reactions people might have to discovering the implications of the position they occupy within the realm of production.[12] Theoretical propositions apart though, in the everyday world, the term *is* used in its psychological sense, is generally and casually used to describe what people have 'thought, felt and wanted at any moment in history and from any point in the class structure'.[13] Working-class autobiography and people's history have been developed as forms that allow the individual and collective expression of these thoughts, feelings and desires about class societies and the effect of class structures on individuals and communities. But as forms of analysis and writing, people's history and working-class autobiography are relatively innocent of psychological theory, and there has been little space within them to discuss the *development* of class-consciousness (as opposed to its expression), nor for understanding of it as a *learned* position, learned in childhood, and often through the exigencies of difficult and lonely lives.

Children present a particular problem here, for whilst some women may learn the official dimensions of class-consciousness by virtue of their entry into the labour market and by adopting forms of struggle and understanding evolved by men,[14] children, who are not located directly within the realm of production, still reach understandings of social position, exclusion and difference. At all levels, class-consciousness must be learned in some way, and we need a model of such a process to explain the social and psychological development of working-class children (indeed, of all children).

When the mental life of working-class women is entered into the realm of production, and their narrative is allowed to disrupt the monolithic story of wage-labour and capital and when childhood and childhood learning are reckoned with, then what makes the old story unsatisfactory is not so much its granite-like *plot*, built around exploiter and exploited, capital and proletariat, but rather its *timing*: the precise how and why of the development of class-consciousness. But if we do allow an unconscious life to working-class children, then we can perhaps see the first loss, the earliest exclusion (known most familiarly to us as the oedipal crisis) brought forward later, and articulated through an adult experience of class and class relations.

An adult experience of class does not in any case, as Sally Alexander has pointed out, 'produce a shared and even consciousness', even if it is fully registered and articulated.[15] This uneven and problematic consciousness (which my mother's life and political conviction represents so clearly) is one of the subjects of this book. A perception of childhood experience and understanding used as the lineaments of adult political analysis, may also help us see under the language and conflicts of class, historically much older articulations – the subjective and political expressions of radicalism – which may still serve to give a voice to people who know that they do not have what they want, who know that they have been cut off from the earth in some way.[16]

The attribution of psychological sameness to the figures in the working-class landscape has been made by men, for whom the transitions of class are at once more ritualized than they are for women, and much harder to make.

Hoggart's description of the plight of the 'scholarship boy' of the thirties and forties, and the particular anxiety afflicting those in the working class

> who have been pulled one stage away from their original culture and have not the intellectual equipment which would then cause them to move on to join the 'declassed' professionals and experts[17]

makes nostalgic reading now in a post-War situation where a whole generation of escapees occupies professional positions that allow them to speak of their working-class origins with authority, to use them, in Seabrook's words 'as a kind of accomplishment'.[18] By the 1950s the divisions of the educational establishment that produced Hoggart's description were much altered and I, a grammar-school girl of the 1960s, was sent to university with a reasonably full equipment of culture and a relative degree of intellectual self-awareness. Jeremy Seabrook, some eight years older than me and at Cambridge in the late fifties, sat with his fellow travellers from working-class backgrounds 'telling each other escape stories, in which we were all picaresque heroes of our own lives'.[19]

But at the University of Sussex in 1965, there were no other women to talk to like this, at least there were none that I met (though as proletarianism was fashionable at the time, there were several men with romantic and slightly untruthful tales to tell). And should I have met a woman like me (there must have been some: we were all children of the Robbins generation), we could not have talked of escape except within a literary framework that we had learned from the working-class novels of the early sixties (some of which, like *Room at the Top*, were set books on certain courses); and that framework was itself ignorant of the material stepping-stones of our escape: clothes, shoes, make-up. We could not be heroines of the conventional narratives of escape. Women are, in the sense that Hoggart and Seabrook present in their pictures of transition, without class, because the cut and fall of a skirt and good leather shoes can take you across the river and to the other side: the fairy-tales tell you that goose-girls may marry kings.

The fixed townscapes of Northampton and Leeds that Hoggart and Seabrook have described show endless streets of houses, where mothers who don't go out to work order the domestic day, where men are masters, and children, when they grow older, express gratitude for the harsh discipline meted out to them. The first task is to particularize this profoundly a-historical landscape (and so this book details a mother who was a working woman and a single parent, and a father who wasn't a patriarch). And once the landscape is detailed and historicized in this way, the urgent need becomes to find a way of theorizing the result of such difference and particularity, not in order to find a description that can be universally applied (the point is *not* to say that all working-class childhoods are the same, nor that experience of them produces unique psychic structures) but so that the people in exile, the inhabitants of the long streets, may start to use the autobiographical 'I', and tell the stories of their life.

*

There are other interpretative devices for my mother which, like working-class autobiographies of childhood, make her no easier to see. Nearly everything that has been written on the subject of mothering (except the literature of pathology, of battering and violence) assumes the desire to mother; and there are feminisms now that ask me to return Persephone-like to my own mother, and find new histories of my strength. When I first came across Kathleen Woodward's *Jipping Street*, I read it with the shocked astonishment of one who had never seen what she knows written down before. Kathleen Woodward's mother of the 1890s was the one I knew: mothers were those who told you how hard it was to have you, how long they were in labour with you ('twenty hours with you', my mother frequently reminded

me) and who told you to accept the impossible contradiction of being both desired and a burden; and not
to complain.[20] This ungiving endurance is admired by
working-class boys who grow up to write about their
mother's flinty courage. But the daughter's silence on the
matter is a measure of the price you pay for survival. I don't
think the baggage will ever lighten, for me or my sister. We
were born, and had no choice in the matter; but we were
burdens, expensive, never grateful enough. There was nothing we could do to pay back the debt of our existence.
'Never have children dear,' she said; 'they ruin your life.'
Shock moves swiftly across the faces of women to whom I
tell this story. But it is *ordinary* not to want your children, I
silently assert; normal to find them a nuisance.

I read the collection *Fathers: Reflections by Daughters*, or
Ann Oakley's *Taking It Like a Woman*[21] and feel the
painful and familiar sense of exclusion from these autobiographies of middle-class little-girlhood and womanhood,
envy of those who belong, who can, like Ann Oakley, use
the outlines of conventional romantic fiction to tell a life
story. And women like this, friends, say: but it was like that
for me too, my childhood was like yours; my father was like
that, my mother didn't want me. What they cannot bear, I
think, is that there exists a poverty and marginality of
experience to which they have no access, structures of
feeling that they have not lived within (and would not want
to live within: for these are the structures of deprivation).
They are caught then in a terrible exclusion, an exclusion
from the experience of others that measures out their own
central relationship to the culture. The myths tell their story,
the fairy-tales show the topography of the houses they once
inhabited. The psychoanalytic drama, which uses the spatial
and temporal structures of all these old tales, permits the
entry of such women to the drama itself. Indeed, the
psychoanalytic drama was constructed to describe that
of middle-class women (and as drama it does of course
describe all such a woman's exclusions, as well as her

relationship to those exclusions, with her absence and all she lacks lying at the very heart of the theory). The woman whose drama psychoanalytic case-study describes in this way never does stand to one side, and watch, and know she doesn't belong.

What follows is largely concerned with how two girl children, growing up in different historical periods, got to be the women they became. The sense of exclusion, of being cut off from what others enjoy, was a dominant sense of both childhoods, but expressed and used differently in two different historical settings. This detailing of social context to psychological development reveals not only difference, but also certain continuities of experience in working-class childhood. For instance, many recent accounts of psychological development and the development of gender, treat our current social situation as astonishingly new and strange:

> On the social/historical level ... we are living in a period in which mothers are increasingly living alone with their children, offering opportunities for new psychic patterns to emerge. Single mothers are forced to make themselves subject to their children; they are forced to invent new symbolic roles ... The child cannot position the mother as object to the father's law, since in single parent households her desire sets things in motion.[22]

But the evidence of some nineteenth- and twentieth-century children used in this book shows that in their own reckoning their households were often those of a single female parent, sometimes because of the passivity of a father's presence, sometimes because of his physical absence. Recent feminisms have often, as Jane Gallop points out in *The Daughter's Seduction*, endowed men with 'the sort of unified phallic sovereignty that characterises an absolute monarch, and which little resembles actual power in our social, economic structure'.[23] We need a reading of history that reveals fathers mattering in a different way from the way they matter in the corpus of traditional psychoanalysis, the novels that depict the same familial settings and in the bourgeois households of the fairy-tales.

A father like mine dictated each day's existence; our lives would have been quite different had he not been there. But he didn't *matter*, and his singular unimportance needs explaining. His not mattering has an effect like this: I don't quite believe in male power; somehow the iron of patriarchy didn't enter into my soul. I accept the idea of male power intellectually, of course (and I will eat my words the day I am raped, or the knife is slipped between my ribs; though I know that will not be the case: in the dreams it is a woman who holds the knife, and only a woman can kill).

Fixing my father, and my mother's mothering, in time and politics can help show the creation of gender in particular households and in particular familial situations at the same time as it demonstrates the position of men and the social reality represented by them in particular households. We need historical accounts of such relationships, not just a longing that they might be different.[24] Above all, perhaps, we need a sense of people's complexity of relationship to the historical situations they inherit. In *Family and Kinship in East London*, the authors found that over half the married women they interviewed had seen their mothers within the preceding twenty-four hours, and that 80 per cent had seen them within the previous week. Young and Willmott assumed that the daughters wanted to do this, and interpreted four visits a week on average as an expression of attachment and devotion.[25] There exists a letter that I wrote to a friend one vacation from Sussex, either in 1966 or in 1967, in which I described my sitting in the evenings with my mother, refusing to go out, holding tight to my guilt and duty, knowing that I *was* her, and that I must keep her company; and we were certainly not Demeter and Persephone to each other, nor ever could be, but two women caught by a web of sexual and psychological relationships in the front room of a council house, the South London streets stretching away outside like the railway lines that brought us and our history to that desperate and silent scene in front of the flickering television screen.

Raymond Williams has written about the difficulty of linking past and present in writing about working-class life, and the result of this difficulty in novels that either show the past`to be a regional zone of experience in which the narrator cancels her present from the situation she is describing, or which are solely about the experience of flight. Writing like this, comments Williams, has lacked 'any sense of the continuity of working class life, which does not cease just because the individual [the writer] moves out of it, but which also itself changes internally'.[26]

This kind of cancellation of a writer's present from the past may take place because novels – stories – work by a process of temporal revelation: they move forward in time in order to demonstrate a state of affairs. The novel that works in this way employs contingency, that is, it works towards the revelation of something not quite certain, but *there*, nevertheless, waiting to be shown by the story,[27] and the story gets told without revealing the shaping force of the writer's current situation.

The highlighting not just of the subject matter of this book, but also of the possibilities of written form it involves, is important, because the construction of the account that follows has something to say about the question that Raymond Williams has raised, and which is largely to do with the writing of stories that aren't central to a dominant culture. My mother cut herself off from the old working class by the process of migration, by retreat from the North to a southern country with my father, hiding secrets in South London's long streets. But she carried with her her childhood, as I have carried mine along the lines of embourgeoisement and state education. In order to outline these childhoods and the uses we put them to, the structure of psychoanalytic case-study – the narrative form that Freud is described as inventing – is used in this book.[28] The written case-study allows the writer to enter the present into the past, allows the dream, the wish or the fantasy of the past to shape current time, and treats them as evidence in their own right. In this way, the narrative form of case-study shows what went into its writing, shows the bits and pieces from which it is made up, in the way that history refuses to do, and that fiction can't.[29] Case-study presents the ebb and flow of memory, the structure of dreams, the stories that people tell to explain themselves to others. The auto-biographical section of this book, the second part, is constructed on such a model.

But something else has to be done with these bits and pieces, with all the tales that are told, in order to take them beyond the point of anecdote and into history. To begin to construct history, the writer has to do two things, make two movements through time. First of all, we need to search backwards from the vantage point of the present in order to appraise things in the past and attribute meaning to them. When events and entities in the past have been given their meaning in this way, then we can trace forward what we have already traced backwards, and make a history.[30] When a history is finally written, events are explained by putting them in causal order and establishing causal connections between them. But what follows in this book does not make a history (even though a great deal of historical material is presented). For a start, I simply do not know enough about many of the incidents described to explain the connections between them. I am unable to perform an act of historical explanation in this way.

This tension between the stories told to me as a child, the diffuse and timeless structure of the case-study with which they are presented, and the compulsions of historical explanation, is no mere rhetorical device. There is a real problem, a real tension here that I cannot resolve (my inability to resolve it is part of the story). All the stories that follow, told as this book tells them, aren't stories in their own right: they exist in tension with other more central ones. In the same way, the processes of working-class autobiography, of people's history and of the working-class novel cannot show a proper and valid culture existing in its own right, underneath the official forms, waiting for revelation. Accounts of working-class life are told by tension and ambiguity, out on the borderlands. The story – my mother's story, a hundred thousand others – cannot be absorbed into the central one: it is both its disruption and its essential counterpoint: this is a drama of *class*.

But visions change, once any story is told; ways of seeing are altered. The point of a story is to present itself momentarily as complete, so that it can be said: it does for now, it will do; it is an account that will last a while. Its point is briefly to make an audience connive in the telling, so that they might say: yes, that's how it was; or, that's how it could have been. So now, the words written down, the world is suddenly full of women waiting, as in Ann Oakley's extraordinary delineation of

> the curiously impressive image of women as always waiting for someone or something, in shopping queues, in antenatal clinics, in bed, for men to come home, at the school gates, by the playground swing, for birth or the growing up of children, in hope of love or freedom or re-employment, waiting for the future to liberate or burden them and the past to catch up with them.[31]

The other side of waiting is wanting. The faces of the women in the queues are the faces of unfulfilled desire; if we look, there are many women driven mad in this way, as my mother was. This is a sad and secret story, but it isn't just hers alone.

*

What historically conscious readers may do with this book is read it as a Lancashire story, see here evidence of a political culture of 1890–1930 carried from the Northwest, to shape another childhood in another place and time.

They will perhaps read it as part of an existing history, seeing here a culture shaped by working women, and their consciousness of themselves as workers. They may see the indefatigable capacity for work that has been described in many other places, the terrifying ability to *get by*, to cope, against all odds. Some historically conscious readers may even find here the irony that this specific social and cultural experience imparted to its women: 'No one gives you anything,' said my mother, as if reading the part of 'our mam' handed to her by the tradition of working-class autobiography. 'If you want things, you have to go out and work for them.' But out of that tradition I can make the dislocation that the irony actually permits, and say: 'If no one will write my story, then I shall have to go out and write it myself.'

The point of being a Lancashire weaver's daughter, as my mother was, is that it is *classy*: what my mother knew was that if you were going to be working class, then you might as well be the best that's going, and for women, Lancashire and weaving provided that elegance, that edge of difference and distinction. I'm sure that she told the titled women whose hands she did when she became a manicurist in the 1960s where it was she came from, proud, defiant: look at me. (Beatrix Campbell has made what I think is a similar point about the classiness of being a miner, for working-class men.)[32]

This is a book about stories; and it is a book about *things* (objects, entities, relationships, people), and the way in which we talk and write about them: about the difficulties of metaphor. Above all, it is about people wanting those things, and the structures of political thought that have labelled this wanting as wrong. Later in the book, suggestions are made about a relatively old structure of political thought in this country, that of radicalism, and its possible entry into the political dialogue of the North-west; and how perhaps it allowed people to feel desire, anger and envy – for the things they did not have.

The things though, will remain a problem. The connection between women and clothes surfaces often in these pages, particularly in the unacknowledged testimony of many nineteenth- and twentieth-century women and girls; and it was with the image of a New Look coat that, in 1950, I made my first attempt to understand and symbolize the content of my mother's desire. I think now of all the stories, all the reading, all the dreams that help us to see ourselves in the landscape, and see ourselves watching as well. 'A woman must continually watch herself,' remarked John Berger some years ago.

> She is almost continually accompanied by her own image of herself. Whilst she is walking across a room or whilst she is weeping at the death of her father, she can scarcely avoid envisioning herself walking and weeping.[33]

This book is intended to specify, in historical terms, some of the processes by which we come to step into the landscape, and see ourselves. But the *clothes* we wear there remain a question. Donald Winnicott wrote about the transitional object (those battered teddies and bits of blanket that babies use in the early stages of distinguishing themselves from the world around them) and its usefulness to the young children who adopt it. The transitional object, he wrote, 'must seem to the infant to give warmth, or to move, or to have texture, or to do something that seems to show it has vitality or reality of its own.'[34] Like clothes: that we may see ourself better as we stand there and watch; and for our protection.

Part two

Exiles

Kay and Gerda sat looking at the picture-book of animals and birds, when just at that moment the clock in the great church-tower struck five. Kay exclaimed: 'Oh dear! I feel as if something had stabbed my heart! And now I've got something into my eye!' . . . 'I think it's gone!' he said; but it was not gone. It was one of the glass pieces from the mirror, the troll mirror, which you no doubt remember, in which everything great and good that was reflected in it became small and ugly, while everything bad and wicked became more distinct and prominent and every fault was at once noticed. Poor Kay had got one of the fragments right into his heart. It would soon become like a lump of ice. It did not cause him any pain, but it was there.

(Hans Christian Andersen, 'The Snow Queen')

The Weaver's Daughter

. . . Stuff slippers and white cotton stockings,
The lasses they mostly do wear,
With a dimity corduroy petticoat,
It is whiter than snow I declare;
With a fringe or a flounce round the bottom
These lasses they will have beside,
And a sash for to go round their middle
And to tie up in bunches behind.

. . . The servant girls follow the fashions,
As well as the best in the place:
They'll dress up their heads like an owl, boys,
And will think it no shame or disgrace.
They will bind up their heads with fine ribbands,
And a large bag of hair hangs behind;
And when they do walk through the streets, boys,
No peacock can touch them for pride.

('The Lasses' Resolution to Follow the Fashion',
c. 1870, in Roy Palmer,
A Touch on the Times: Songs of Social Change,
1770–1914, Penguin, 1974)

When I was three, before my sister was born, I had a dream. It remains quite clear across the years, the topography absolutely plain, so precise in details of dress that I can use them to place the dream in historical time. We were in a street, the street so wide and the houses so distant across the road that it might not have been a street at all; and the

houses lay low with gaps between them, so that the sky filled
a large part of the picture. Here, at the front, on this side of
the wide road, a woman hurried along, having crossed from
the houses behind. The perspective of the dream must have
shifted several times, for I saw her once as if from above,
moving through a kind of square, or crossing-place, and
then again from the fixed point of the dream where I stood
watching her, left forefront.

She wore the New Look, a coat of beige gaberdine which
fell in two swaying, graceful pleats from her waist at the
back (the swaying must have come from very high heels, but
I didn't notice her shoes), a hat tipped forward from hair
swept up at the back. She hurried, something jerky about
her movements, a nervous, agitated walk, glancing round at
me as she moved across the foreground. Several times she
turned and came some way back towards me, admonishing,
shaking her finger.

Encouraging me to follow in this way perhaps, but moving too fast for me to believe that this was what she wanted,
she entered a revolving door of dark, polished wood, mahogany and glass, and started to go round and round, looking
out at me as she turned. I wish I knew what she was doing,
and what she wanted me to do.

In childhood, only the surroundings show, and nothing is
explained. Children do not possess a social analysis of what
is happening to them, or around them, so the landscape and
the pictures it presents have to remain a background, taking
on meaning later, from different circumstances. That dream
is the past that lies at the heart of my present: it is my
interpretative device, the means by which I can tell a story.
My understanding of the dream built up in layers over a long
period of time. Its strange lowered vista for instance, which
now reminds the adult more than anything else of George
Herriman's 'Krazy Kat'[1] where buildings disappear and
reappear from frame to frame, seems an obvious representation of London in the late forties and early fifties: all the
houses had gaps in between because of the bombs, and the

sky came closer to the ground than seemed right. I understood what I had seen in the dream when I learned the words 'gaberdine' and 'mahogany'; and I was born in the year of the New Look, and understood by 1951 and the birth of my sister, that dresses needing twenty yards for a skirt were items as expensive as children – more expensive really, because after 1948 babies came relatively cheap, on tides of free milk and orange juice, but good cloth in any quantity was hard to find for a very long time.

Detail like this provides retrospective labelling; but it is not evidence about a period of historical time. The only *evidence* that the dream offers is the feeling of childhood – all childhoods, probably – the puzzlement of the child watching from the pavement, wondering what's going on, what they, the adults, are up to, what they want from you, and what they expect you to do. It is evidence in this way, because as an area of feeling it is brought forward again and again to shape responses to quite different events. Memory alone cannot resurrect past time, because it is memory itself that shapes it, long after historical time has passed. The dream is not a fixed event of the summer of 1950; it has passed through many stages of use and exploration, and such reinterpretation gives an understanding that the child at the time can't possess: it's only recently that I've come to see who the woman in the New Look coat actually was.

Now, later, I see the time of my childhood as a point between two worlds: an older 'during the War', 'before the War', 'in the Depression', 'then'; and the place we inhabit now. The War was so palpable a presence in the first five years of my life that I still find it hard to believe that I didn't live through it. There were bomb-sites everywhere, prefabs on waste land, most things still on points, my mother tearing up the ration book when meat came off points, over my sister's pram, outside the library in the High Street in the summer of 1951, a gesture that still fills me with the desire to do something so defiant and final; and then looking across the street at a woman wearing a full-skirted dress, and then down at the forties straight-skirted navy blue suit she was still wearing, and longing, irritatedly, for the New Look; and then at us, the two living barriers to twenty yards of cloth. Back home, she said she'd be able to get it at the side door of the mill; but not here; not with you two . . .

My mother's story was told to me early on, in bits and pieces throughout the fifties, and it wasn't delivered to entertain, like my father's much later stories were, but rather to teach me lessons. There was a child, an eleven-year-old from a farm seven miles south of Coventry, sent off to be a maid-of-all-work in a parsonage in Burnley. She had her tin trunk, and she cried, waiting on the platform with her family seeing her off, for the through train to Manchester. They'd sent her fare, the people in Burnley; 'But think how she felt, such a little girl, she was only eleven, with nothing but her little tin box. Oh, she did cry.' I cry now over accounts of childhoods like this, weeping furtively over the reports of nineteenth-century commissions of inquiry into child labour, abandoning myself to the luxuriance of grief in libraries, tears staining the pages where Mayhew's little watercress girl tells her story. The lesson was, of course, that I must never, ever, cry for myself, for I was a lucky little girl: my tears should be for all the strong, brave women who gave me life. This story, which embodied fierce resentment against the unfairness of things, was carried through seventy years and three generations, and all of them, all the good women, dissolved into the figure of my mother, who was, as she told us, *a good mother*. She didn't go out dancing or drinking (gin, mother's ruin, was often specified. 'Your mother drank gin once,' my father told me years later, with nostalgic regret). She didn't go, as one mother she'd known, in a story of maternal neglect that I remember thinking was over the top at the time, and tie a piece of string round my big toe, dangle it through the window and down the front of the house, so that the drunken mother, returning from her carousing, she could tug at it, wake the child, get the front door open and send it down the shop for a basin of pie and peas. I still put myself to sleep by thinking about *not* lying on a cold pavement covered with newspapers.

The eleven-year-old who cried on Coventry station hated being a servant. She got out as soon as she could and found work in the weaving sheds – 'she was a good weaver; six looms under her by the time she was sixteen' – married, produced nine children, eight of whom emigrated to the cotton mills of Massachusetts before the First World War, managed, 'never went before the Guardians'.[2] It was much, much later that I learned from *One Hand Tied Behind Us* that four was the usual number of looms in Lancashire weaving towns.[3] Burnley weavers were badly organized over the question of loom supervision, and my great-grandmother had six not because she was a good weaver, but because she was exploited. In 1916, when her daughter Carrie's husband was killed at the Somme, she managed that too, looking after the three-year-old, my mother, so that Carrie could go on working at the mill.

But long before the narrative fell into place, before I could dress the eleven-year-old of my imagination in the clothing of the 1870s, I knew perfectly well what that child had done, and how she had felt. She cried, because tears are cheap; and then she stopped, and got by, because no one gives you anything in this world. What was given to her, passed on to all of us, was a powerful and terrible endurance, the self-destructive defiance of those doing the best they can with what life hands out to them.

From a cotton town, my mother had a heightened aware-ness of fabric and weave, and I can date events by the clothes I wore as a child, and the material they were made of. Post-War children had few clothes, because of rationing, but not only scarcity, rather names like barathea, worsted, gaberdine, twill, jersey, lawn . . . fix them in my mind. The dream of the New Look must have taken place during or after the summer of 1950, because in it I wore one of my two summer dresses, one of green, one of blue gingham, which were made that year and which lasted me, with letting down, until I went to school.

Sometime during 1950, I think before the summer, before the dresses were made, I was taken north to Burnley and into the sheds, where one afternoon my mother visited someone she used to know as a child, now working there. The woman smiled and nodded at me, through the noise that made a surrounding silence. Afterwards, my mother told me that they had to lip-read: they couldn't hear each other speak for the noise of the looms. But I didn't notice the noise. The woman wore high platform-soled black shoes that I still believe I heard click on the bright polished floor as she walked between her looms. Whenever I hear the word 'tending' I always think of that confident attentiveness to the needs of the machines, the control over work that was unceasing, with half a mind and hands engaged, but the looms always demanding attention. When I worked as a primary-school teacher I sometimes retrieved that feeling with a particular clarity, walking between the tables on the hard floor, all the little looms working, but needing my constant adjustment.

The woman wore a dress that seemed very short when I recalled the picture through the next few years: broad shoulders, a straight skirt patterned with black and red flowers that hung the way it did – I know now – because it had some rayon in it. The post-War years were full of women longing for a full skirt and unable to make it. I wanted to walk like that, a short skirt, high heels, bright red lipstick, in charge of all that machinery.

This was the first encounter with the landscape of my mother's past. We came once again, on the last trip I made North before I was nineteen, during the autumn or winter of 1950 when, as I can now work out, my mother was pregnant with my sister. On this particular and first visit of the late spring, the world was still clear. On the edge of the town, it seemed like the top of the street, a little beck ran through some woods, with bluebells growing there, so that memory can tell that it was May. We paddled in the shallow water; this was the clean water that they used to use for the cotton; it came from another place, where the mills were before there was steam; you could see the gravel clear beneath. We didn't pick the flowers: we left them there for other people to enjoy. She wore her green tweed jacket; it was lucky she didn't have any stockings on otherwise she'd only have had to take them off; she laughed, she smiled: the last time.

At the back of the house, through the yard to the lane, the lavatory was perched over another stream; you could see the water running past if you looked down. In this back lane I played with another child, older than me, she was four: Maureen. She was a Catholic, my grandmother said, but I could play with her, she was a nice little girl, but they weren't like us: you could tell them by their eyes. It was the women who told you about the public world, of work and politics, the details of social distinction. My grandmother's lodger, the man who was to become her third husband when his wife died ten years later, stayed self-effacingly in the background as she explained these things. Anti-Catholicism propelled my mother's placing of herself in a public sphere. A few years later she often repeated the story of Molly, her best friend at school, the priest beckoning to the Catholic child from over the road, furtively passing a betting slip; the strain of the penny collections at church with a dozen mouths to feed at home.

As a teenage worker my mother had broken with a recently established tradition and on leaving school in 1927 didn't go into the sheds. She lied to me though when, at about the age of eight, I asked her what she'd done, and she said she'd worked in an office, done clerical work. Ten years later, on my third and last visit to Burnley and practising the accomplishments of the oral historian, I talked to my grandmother and she, puzzled, told me that Edna had never worked in any office, had in fact been apprenticed to a dry-cleaning firm that did tailoring and mending. On that same visit, the first since I was four, I found a reference written by the local doctor for my mother who, about 1930, applied for a job as a ward-maid at the local asylum, confirming that she was clean, strong, honest and intelligent. I wept over that, of course, for a world where some people might doubt her – my – cleanliness. I didn't care much about the honesty, and I knew I was strong; but there are people everywhere waiting for you to slip up, to show signs of dirtiness and stupidity, so that they can send you back where you belong.

She didn't finish her apprenticeship – I deduce that, rather than know it – sometime, it must have been 1934, came South, worked in Woolworth's on the Edgware Road, spent the War years in Roehampton, a ward-maid again, in the hospital where they mended fighter pilots' ruined faces. Now I can feel the deliberate vagueness in her accounts of those years: 'When did you meet daddy?' – 'Oh, at a dance, at home.' There were no photographs. Who came to London first? I wish now that I'd asked that question. He worked on the buses when he arrived, showed me a canopy in front of a hotel once, that he'd pulled down on his first solo drive. He was too old to be called up (a lost generation of men who were too young for the first War, too old for the second). There's a photograph of him standing in front of the cabbages he'd grown for victory, wearing his Home Guard uniform. But what did he *do* after his time on the buses, and during the War years? Too late now to find out.

*

During the post-War housing shortage my father got an office job with a property company, and the flat to go with it. I was born in March 1947, at the peak of the Bulge, more babies born that month than ever before or after, and carried through the terrible winter of 1946–7. We moved to Streatham Hill in June 1951, to an estate owned by the same company (later to be taken over by Lambeth Council), and a few years after the move my father got what he wanted, which was to be in charge of the company's boiler maintenance. On his death certificate it says 'heating engineer'.

In the 1950s my mother took in lodgers. Streatham Hill Theatre (now a bingo hall) was on the pre-West End circuit, and we had chorus girls staying with us for weeks at a time. I was woken up in the night sometimes, the spare bed in my room being made up for someone they'd met down the Club, the other lodger's room already occupied. I like the idea of being the daughter of a theatrical landlady, but that enterprise, in fact, provides me with my most startling and problematic memories. The girl from Aberdeen really did say 'Och, no, not on the table!' as my father flattened a bluebottle with his hand, but did he *really* put down a newspaper at the same table to eat his breakfast? I remember it happening, but it's so much like the books that I feel a fraud, a bit-part player in a soft and southern version of *The Road to Wigan Pier*.

I remember incidents like these, I think, because I was about seven, the age at which children start to notice social detail and social distinction, but also more particularly because the long lesson in hatred for my father had begun, and the early stages were in the traditional mode, to be found in the opening chapters of *Sons and Lovers* and Lawrence's description of the inculcated dislike of Mr Morrell, of female loathing for coarse male habits. The newspaper on the table is problematic for me because it was problematic for my mother, a symbol of all she'd hoped to escape and all she'd landed herself in. (It was at this time, I think, that she told me that her own mother, means-tested in the late 1920s, had won the sympathy of the Relieving Officer, who ignored the presence of the saleable piano because she kept a clean house, with a cloth on the table.)

Now, thirty years later, I feel a great regret for the father of my first four years, who took me out and who probably loved me, irresponsibly ('It's alright for him; he doesn't have to look after you'), and I wish I could tell him now, even though he really was a sod, that I'm sorry for the years of rejection and dislike. But we were forced to choose, early on, which side we belonged to, and children have to come down on the side that brings the food home and gets it on the table. By 1955 I was beginning to hate him – because *he* was to blame, for the lack of money, for my mother's terrible dissatisfaction at the way things were working out.

Changes in the market place, the growth of real income and the proliferation of consumer goods that marked the mid-1950s, were used by my mother to measure out her discontent: there existed a newly expanding and richly endowed material world in which she was denied a place. The new consumer goods came into the house slowly, and we were taught to understand that our material deprivations were due entirely to my father's meanness. We had the first fridge in our section of the street (which he'd got cheap, off the back of a lorry, contacts in the trade) but were very late to acquire a television. I liked the new vacuum cleaner at first, because it meant no longer having to do the stairs with a stiff brush. But in fact it added to my Saturday work because I was expected to clean more with the new machine. Now I enjoy shocking people by telling them how goods were introduced into households under the guise of gifts for children: the fridge in the house of the children we played with over the road was given to the youngest as a birthday present – the last thing an eight-year-old wants. My mother laughed at this, scornfully: the clothes and shoes she gave us as birthday presents were conventional gifts for all post-War children, but the record player also came into the house in this way, as my eleventh birthday present. I wasn't allowed to take it with me when I left, though: it really wasn't mine at all.

What happened at school was my own business, no questions ever asked, no encouragement nor discouragement ever given. It became just the thing I did, like my mother's going out to work. Later, the material conditions for educational success were provided: a table in my room, a pattern of domestic work that allowed homework to be done. From the earliest time I was expected to be competent: to iron a blouse, scrub a floor, learn to read, pass an exam; and I was. (There was, though, as my sister was to discover later, all hell to pay if you failed.) Indifference to what happened at school was useful: learning is the one untouched area of my life. So in reconstructing the pattern of this neglect, I am surprised to find myself walking up the hill with my mother from school one afternoon. She was smiling a pleased smile, and working things out, I think it must have been 1956, the day she was told that I'd be going into the eleven-plus class and so (because everyone in the class passed the exam) would be going to grammar school. I remember the afternoon because I asked her what class we were; or rather, I asked her if we were middle class, and she was evasive. I answered my own question, said I thought we must be middle class, and reflected very precisely in that moment on my mother's black, waisted coat with the astrakhan collar, and her high-heeled black suede shoes, her lipstick. She looked so much better than the fat, spreading, South London mothers around us, that I thought we had to be middle class.

The coat and the lipstick came from her own work. 'If you want something, you have to go out and work for it. Nobody gives you anything; nothing comes free in this world.' About 1956 or 1957 she got an evening job in one of the espresso bars opening along the High Road, making sandwiches and frying eggs. She saved up enough money to take a manicuring course and in 1958 got her diploma, thus achieving a certified skill for the first time in her forty-five years. When I registered her death I was surprised to find myself giving 'manicurist' as her trade, for the possibility of a trade was something she seemed to have left behind in the North. She always worked in good places, in the West End; the hands she did were in *Vogue* once. She came home with stories and imitations of her 'ladies'. She told me how she 'flung' a sixpenny piece back at a titled woman who'd given it her as a tip: 'If you can't afford any more than that

Madam, I suggest you keep it.' Wonderful! – like tearing up the ration books.

She knew where we stood in relation to this world of privilege and possession, had shown me the place long before, in the bare front bedroom where the health visitor spoke haughtily to her. Many women have stood thus, at the window, looking out, their children watching their exclusion: 'I remember as it were but yesterday,' wrote Samuel Bamford in 1849, 'after one of her visits to the dwelling of that "fine lady"' (his mother's sister, who had gone up in the world):

> she divested herself of her wet bonnet, her soaked shoes, and changed her dripping outer garments and stood leaning with her elbow on the window sill, her hand up to her cheek, her eyes looking upon vacancy and the tears trickling over her fingers.[4]

What we learned now, in the early 1960s, through the magazines and anecdotes she brought home, was how the goods of that world of privilege might be appropriated, with the cut and fall of a skirt, a good winter coat, with leather shoes, a certain voice; but above all with clothes, the best boundary between you and a cold world.

It was at this time that her voice changed, and her Lancashire accent began to disappear. Earlier, years before, she'd entertained us in the kitchen by talking really broad, not her natural dialect but a stagey variety that always preceded a rapid shift to music-hall cockney for a rendering of 'She Was Only a Bird in a Gilded Cage':

> It's the same the whole world over
> Ain't it a bleeding shame
> It's the rich what gets the pleasure,
> It's the poor what gets the blame.

*

We weren't, I now realize by doing the sums, badly off. My father paid the rent, all the bills, gave us our pocket money, and a fixed sum of seven pounds a week housekeeping money, quite a lot in the late 1950s[5] went on being handed over every Friday until his death, even when estrangement was obvious, and he was living most of the time with somebody else. My mother must have made quite big money in tips, for the records of her savings, no longer a secret, show quite fabulous sums being stored away in the early 1960s. When she died there was over £40,000 in building-society accounts. Poverty hovered as a belief. It existed in stories of the thirties, in a family history. Even now when a bank statement comes in that shows I'm overdrawn or when the gas bill for the central heating seems enormous, my mind turns to quite inappropriate strategies, like boiling down the ends of soap, and lighting fires with candle ends and spills of screwed up newspaper to save buying wood. I think about these things because they were domestic economies that we practised in the 1950s. We believed we were badly off because we children were expensive items, and all these arrangements had been made for us. 'If it wasn't for you two,' my mother told us, 'I could be off somewhere else.' After going out manicuring she started spending Sunday afternoons in bed, and we couldn't stay in the house or play on the doorstep for fear of disturbing her. The house was full of her terrible tiredness and her terrible resentment; and I knew it was all my fault.

Later, in 1977, after my father's death, we found out that they were never married, that we were illegitimate. In 1934 my father left his wife and two-year-old daughter in the North, and came to London. He and my mother had been together for at least ten years when I was born, and we think now that I was her hostage to fortune, the factor that might persuade him to get a divorce and marry her. But the ploy failed.

Just before my mother's death, playing about with the photographs on the front bedroom mantelpiece, my niece discovered an old photograph under one of me at three. A woman holds a tiny baby. It's the early 1930s, a picture of the half-sister left behind. But I think I knew about her and her mother long before I looked them both in the face, or heard about their existence, knew that the half-understood adult conversations around me, the two trips to Burnley in 1951, the quarrels about 'her', the litany of 'she', 'she', 'she' from behind closed doors, made up the figure in the New Look coat, hurrying away, wearing the clothes that my mother wanted to wear, angry with me yet nervously inviting me to follow, caught finally in the revolving door. We have proper birth certificates, because my mother must have told a simple lie to the registrar, a discovery about the verisimilitude of documents that worries me a lot as a historian.

*

What kind of secret was the illegitimacy? It was a real secret, that is, the product of an agreed silence on the part of two people about a real event (or absence of event), and it was an extremely well-kept secret. Yet it revealed itself at the time. Often, before I found out about it in 1977 and saw the documents, the sense of my childhood that I carried through the years was that people knew something about me, something that was wrong with me, that I didn't know myself. The first dramatic enactment of the idea that I should not embarrass people with my presence came in 1954 when the children we played with in the street suggested that I go to Sunday school with them. It is a measure of the extreme isolation of our childhood that this event took on the status of entering society itself. Tremulous for days, I then stood reluctantly on the doorstep after Sunday dinner when they called for me, clutching the hot, acrid penny that I'd been told I'd need for the collection, saying: they might not want me to come; they won't want me. From inside the house I was told to stop making a fuss and get up the road. It was a High Anglican church. We were given a little book with space for coloured stamps showing scenes from the Gospels that you received for each attendance.

Every stamp cries duty done
Every blank cries shame;
Finish what you have begun
In the Saviour's name

exhorted the book inside the front cover (a familiar
message; the first social confirmation of the structures of
endurance that the domestic day imparted). I stayed to win
many Church of England hymnals.

It wasn't I think, the legal impropriety that I knew about,
the illegitimacy; rather I felt the wider disjuncture of our
existence, its lack of authorization.

*

In 1954 the *Pirates of Penzance* was playing at the
Streatham Hill Theatre, and we had one of the baritones as a
lodger instead of the usual girls. He was different from
them, didn't eat in the kitchen with us, but had my mother
bake him potatoes and grate carrots which he ate in the
isolation of the dining-room. He converted my mother to
Food Reform, and when she made a salad of grated vegetables for Christmas dinner in 1955, my father walked out
and I wished he'd taken us with him.

I've talked to other people whose mothers came to natur-
opathy in the 1950s, and it's been explained as a way of
eating posh for those who didn't know about continental
food. I think it did have a lot to do with the status that being
different conferred, for in spite of the austerity of our
childhood, we believed that we were better than other
people, the food we ate being a mark of this, because our
mother told us so – so successfully that even now I have to
work hard at actually seeing the deprivations. But much
more than difference, our diet had to do with the need,
wrenched from restricted circumstances, to be in charge of
the body. Food Reform promised an end to sickness if
certain procedures were followed, a promise that was not,
of course, fulfilled. I spent a childhood afraid to fall ill,

because being ill would mean that my mother would have to stay off work and lose money.

But more fundamental than this, I think, a precise costing of our childhood lay behind our eating habits. Brussel sprouts, baked potatoes, grated cheese, the variation of vegetables in the summer, a tin of vegetarian steak pudding on Sundays and a piece of fruit afterwards is a monotonous but healthy diet, and I can't think of many cheaper ways to feed two children and feel you're doing your best for them at the same time. We can't ever have cost very much. She looked at us sometimes, after we'd finished eating. 'Good, Kay, eh?' What I see on her face now is a kind of muted satisfaction; she'd done her best, though her best was limited: not her fault. Children she'd grown up with had died in the 1930s: 'They hadn't enough to eat.'

She brought the food home at night, buying each day's supply when she got off the bus from work. My sister's job was to meet her at the bus-stop with the wheel basket so she didn't have to carry the food up the road. We ate a day's supply at a time, so there was never much in the house overnight except bread for breakfast and the staples that were bought on Saturday. When I started to think about these things I was in a position to interpret this way of living and eating as a variation of the spending patterns of poverty described in Booth's and Rowntree's great surveys at the turn of the century; but now I am sure that it was the cheapness of it that propelled the practice. We were a finely balanced investment, threatening constantly to topple over into the realm of demand and expenditure. I don't think, though, that until we left home we ever cost more to feed and clothe than that seven pounds handed over each week.

Now I see the pattern of our nourishment laid down, like our usefulness, by an old set of rules. At six I was old enough to go on errands, at seven to go further to pay the rent and the rates, go on the long dreary walk to the Co-op for the divi. By eight I was old enough to clean the house and do the weekend shopping. At eleven it was understood that I washed the breakfast things, lit the fire in the winter and scrubbed the kitchen floor before I started my homework. At fifteen, when I could legally go out to work, I got a Saturday job which paid for my clothes (except my school uniform, which was part of the deal, somehow). I think that until I drop I will clean wherever I happen to be on Saturday morning. I take a furtive and secret pride in the fact that I can do all these things, that I am physically strong, can lift and carry things that defeat other women, wonder with some scorn what it must be like to learn to clean a house when adult, and not to have the ability laid down as part of the growing self. Like going to sleep by contrasting a bed with a pavement, I sometimes find myself thinking that if the worst comes to the worst, I can always earn a living by my hands; I can scrub, clean, cook and sew: all you have in the end is your labour.

I was a better deal than my sister, because I passed the eleven plus, went to grammar school, would get a good job, marry a man who would in her words 'buy me a house and you a house. There's no virtue in poverty.' In the mid-1960s the Sunday colour supplements were full of pictures of student life, and she came to see a university as offering the same arena of advantage as the good job had earlier done. The dreary curtailment of our childhood was, we discovered after my mother's death, the result of the most fantastic saving: for a house, the house that was never bought. When I was about seventeen I learned that V. S. Naipaul had written *A House for Mr Biswas* in Streatham Hill, a few streets away from where we lived. There are interpretations now that ask me to see the house, both the fictional one and the one my mother longed for through the years, as the place of undifferentiated and anonymous desire, to see it standing in her dream as the objects of the fairy-tales do – princesses, golden geese, palaces – made desirable in the story simply because someone wants them.[6] But for my mother, as for Mr Biswas, the house was valuable in itself because of what it represented of the social world: a place of safety, wealth and position, a closed door, a final resting place. It was a real dream that dictated the pattern of our days.

It seems now to have been a joyless childhood. There were neighbours who fed us meat and sweets, sorry for us, tea parties we went to that we were never allowed to return. I recall the awful depression of Sunday afternoons, my mother with a migraine in the front bedroom, the house an absolute stillness. But I don't *remember* the oddness; it's a reconstruction. What I remember is what I read, and playing Annie Oakley by myself all summer long in the recreation ground, running up and down the hill in my brown gingham dress, wearing a cowboy hat and carrying a rifle. Saturday-morning pictures confirmed it all: women worked hard, earned their own living; carried guns into the bargain.

The essence of being a good child is taking on the perspective of those who are more powerful than you, and I was good in this way as my sister never was. A house up the road, Sunday afternoon 1958, plates of roast lamb offered. My sister ate, but I refused; not out of sacrifice, nor because I was resisting temptation (I firmly believed that meat would make me ill, as my mother said) but because I understood (though this is the adult's formulation rather than the ten-year-old's) that the price of the meal was condemnation of my mother's oddness, and I wasn't having that. I was a very upright child.

At eight I had my first migraine (I could not please her; I might as well join her; they stopped soon after I left home) and I started to get rapidly and relentlessly short-sighted. I literally stopped seeing for a very long time. It is through the development of symptoms like these, some of them neurotic, that I can site the disasters of our childhood, and read it from an outsider's point of view. I think I passed those years believing that we were unnoticed, *unseen*; but of course we were seen, and the evidence of witnesses was retrievable by memory much later on. In 1956 when the first migraine opened a tunnel of pain one June morning, my little sister developed acute psoriasis. My teacher was worried at my

failing sight, I couldn't see the board by the spring of 1957
and read a book under my desk during arithmetic lessons.
Did he send a note to my mother? Surely he must have done;
what else could have shaken her conviction that glasses
would be bad for me? He said to me the morning after he'd
seen her, 'Your mother says you're doing exercises for your
eyes; make sure you do them properly.' I thought he was
being kind, and he was; but I preserved the voice that I might
later hear the disapproval in it. I think they must have used
the eleven-plus and the amount of blackboard work it
involved as a lever, because I got a pair of glasses before the
exam.

That afternoon she walked up the road with me, what had
they told her? The next year, standing by my new teacher's
desk, now in the eleven-plus class, he showed my book to
what must have been a student on teaching practice. 'This
one,' he said, 'has an inferiority complex.' I didn't understand, had no dictionary in which to look up the words, but
preserved them by my own invented syllabary, rehearsing
them, to bring out for much later scrutiny. I must in fact
have known that people were watching, being witnesses, for
some years later I started to play a game of inviting their
comment and disapproval and then withdrawing the spec-
tacle I had placed before their eyes, making them feel
ashamed of the pity they had felt. By the time I was fifteen
we'd all three of us given up, huddled with tiredness and
irritation in the house where my father was only now an
intermittent presence. The house was a tip; none of us did
any housework any more; broken china wasn't replaced; at
meal times my mother, my sister and I shared the last knife
between us. Responsible now for my own washing, I scarcely did any, spent the winter changing about the layers of five
petticoats I wore to keep warm, top to bottom through the
cold months. One morning, asked by the games mistress
why I wasn't wearing my school blouse, I said I hadn't been
able to find it in the place I'd put it down the night before
(not true; I hadn't a clean one), presenting thus a scene of

baroque household disorganization, daring her to disapprove, hoping she would.

Ten years before this, school had taught me to read, and I found out for myself how to do it fast. By the time I was six I read all the time, rapidly and voraciously. You couldn't join the library until you were seven, and before that I read my Hans Christian Andersen from back to front when I'd read it from start to finish. Kay was my name at home, and I knew that Kay, the boy in 'The Snow Queen', was me, who had a lump of ice in her heart. I knew that one day I might be asked to walk on the edge of knives, like the Little Mermaid, and was afraid that I might not be able to bear the pain. Foxe's *Book of Martyrs* was in the old library, a one-volume edition with coloured illustrations for Victorian children, the text pruned to a litany of death by flame. My imagination was furnished with the passionate martyrdom of the Protestant North '. . . Every blank cries shame; Finish what you have begun, In the Saviour's name.'

I see now the relentless laying down of guilt, and I feel a faint surprise that I must interpret it that way. My sister, younger than me, with children of her own and perhaps thereby with a clearer measure of what we lacked, tells me to recall a mother who never played with us, whose eruptions from irritation into violence were the most terrifying of experiences; and she is there, the figure of nightmares, though I do find it difficult to think about in this way. Such reworking of past time is new, infinitely surprising; and against it I must balance what it felt like then, and the implications of the history given me in small doses; that not being hungry and having a warm bed to lie in at night, I had a good childhood, was better than other people; was a *lucky* little girl.

*

My mother had wanted to marry a king. That was the best of my father's stories, told in the pub in the 1960s, of how difficult it had been to live with her in 1937, during the

Abdication months. Mrs Simpson was no prettier than her, no more clever than her, no better than her. It wasn't fair that a king should give up his throne for her, and not for the weaver's daughter. From a traditional Labour background, my mother rejected the politics of solidarity and communality, always voted Conservative, for the left could not embody her desire for things to be *really* fair, for a full skirt that took twenty yards of cloth, for a half-timbered cottage in the country, for the prince who did not come. For my mother, the time of my childhood was the place where the fairy-tales failed.

A Thin Man

Roll up, roll up, come and see the mermaid,
See the lovely lady, half a woman, half a fish.
In went the lads to show it wasn't swank,
When little Tommy 'Iggins put some whisky in the
    tank.
Well, she got frisky, swimmin' in the whisky,
And when she come up for air
She bowed to the audience, gave 'er tail a swish;
'Er tail it come off, and she really looked delish;
She says, 'What d'y'want, lads, a bit o' meat or
    fish?'
At the Rawtenstall Annual Fair.

('Rawtenstall Annual Fair', 1932, from Roy
Palmer, *A Ballad History of England*,
Batsford, 1979)

By the time my father could sit down in a pub with me,
slightly drunk, tell me and my friends about Real Life, crack
a joke about a Pakistani that silenced a whole table once,
and talk about the farm labourer's – his grandfather's –
journey up from Eye in Suffolk working on the building
of the Great North Western Railway, up to Rawtenstall on
the Lancashire–Yorkshire border, I was doing history at
Sussex, and knew more than he did about the date and
timing of journeys like that. My father, old but gritty,
glamorous in the eyes of the class of '68, a South London
wide boy with an authentic background, described his

grandfather's funeral, about 1912, when a whole other family – wife, children, grandchildren – turned up out of the blue from somewhere further down the line, where they'd been established on the navvy's journey north. (This was a circumstance paralleled at his own funeral, when the friends and relations of the woman he'd been living with for part of the week since the early 1960s stole the show from us, the pathetic huddle of the family of his middle years.)

When I look in the mirror, I see her face, but I know in fact that I look more like him. A real Lancashire face. He was a thin man. I knew his height, five foot ten, but he never seemed tall; he shrank in later years to not much above my height. The silhouette of men has changed completely since the 1950s, and it is this above all else that has altered the outlines of city streets; not the shape of the buildings nor the absence of trams and the growing sleekness of cars, but the fact that men no longer wear hats – broad-brimmed felt hats, tipped slightly over one eye. The Sandeman port man loomed on the hoardings outside Hammersmith Broadway station, the first thing I can remember, sitting up in my pram: an exaggeration and extrapolation of how they all looked, huge coat swirling, trousers flapping, the broad-brimmed rakish hat. A consistent point of my mother's propaganda against him was the shoddiness of his dress and the cheapness of his clothes, his awful ties, his refusal to spend money on his appearance, his lack of taste. But memory doesn't detail him like that; rather, a silhouette, a dapper outline.

*

He took me out once to a bluebell wood. My sister had just been born, we were waiting to move to Streatham Hill: spring 1951. I wore one of the two gingham dresses (I can't remember which colour, I can never remember the colour; they are both just the dress, the clothing of dreams). He was to take me out again, but this time in the bluebell wood was really the last time. I had a sister; we were about to move; his expulsion from the domestic scene about to begin.

It was shaded, a real wood, the sunlight outside beyond the trees, with a fern-covered slope up to the left of the path, the bluebells growing up the slope, and a clearing at the top of that. Up this small incline, and my father started to pick the bluebells from in between the ferns, making a bunch. Did he give me some to hold? I can't remember, except how else to know about their white watery roots, the pale cleanness pulled from the earth? And if he did give me some, what did I do with them in the next few minutes?

The arrival of the forest-keeper was a dramatic eruption on this scene, jarring colour descending on a shady place, a hairy jacket in that strange orange tweed that park-keepers still sometimes wear, plus-fours, brown boots and a pork-pie hat. He was angry with my father, shouted at him: it wasn't allowed. Hadn't he read the notice, there'd be no bluebells left if people pulled them up by the roots. He snatched the bunch from my father's hand, scattered the flowers over the ground and among the ferns, their white roots glimmering, unprotected; and I thought: yes; he doesn't know how to pick bluebells.

My father stood, quite vulnerable in memory now. He was a thin man. I wonder if I remember the waisted and pleated flannel trousers of the early 1950s because in that confrontation he was the loser, feminized, outdone? They made him appear thinner, and because of the way the ground sloped, the forest-keeper, very solid and powerful, was made to appear taller than him. In remembering this scene I always forget, always have to deliberately call to mind the fact that my father retaliated, shouted back; and that we then retreated, made our way back down the path, the tweed man the victor, watching our leaving.

All the charity I possess lies in that moment. Any account that presents its subjects as cold, or shivering or in any way unprotected recalls the precise structure of its feeling. The child who told Henry Mayhew about her life as a seller of cresses in the winter of 1850 stands on the page clutching her shawl about her thin shoulders as the very aetiology of my pity. And there is a more difficult charity that lies somewhere beneath this structure, partly obscured by figures of the imagination like the little watercress girl: pity for something that at the age of four I knew and did not know about my father (know now, and do not know), something about the roots and their whiteness, and the way in which they had been pulled away, to wither exposed on the bank.

Summer came, and we started to live in the new house. It was June, a hot afternoon out in the garden, which was soon to become a farmyard of hen-houses and duck-ponds made out of old tin baths, but now on this hot day, a couple of weeks after we'd moved from Hammersmith, the perfect and sedate little garden made by the old couple who inhabited the house for forty years. The world went wrong that afternoon: there is evidence: a photograph. My father said 'Smile, Kay,' and I smiled; but it is really the day of my first dislocation. I lie on my stomach on the grass, my baby sister on a rug to my right, just in front of me. I am irritated and depressed because she has come to stay. Things have changed: on removal day I turned on the kitchen tap to fill a cup with water and couldn't turn it off, and the removal man was angry with me: the first time an adult's anger has been directed at me. I remember this now. Somewhere on the grass, beyond the photograph, is an apple that I've been given to cheer me up, but that I refuse to eat. We carry moments like this through a lifetime: things were wrong; there was a dislocation between me and the world; I am not inside myself. And he said 'Smile Kay,' and I smiled: the first deception, the first lie.

*

He had a story about how he left the North, a good story, well told. He'd had a few when he first presented it to me, and listeners from that Christmas meeting of 1967 in the pub remember its inconsistencies above anything else. The setting for the tale my father tells is the Blackpool Tower ballroom, it's the summer, and Robin Richmond is playing the organ. Which year? My calculation now says it must be 1934, but he doesn't mention dates himself. Is the famous organist introduced to add glamour to the occasion and the telling of it, even though my father affects to despise the sea-side medleys he's playing? Then suddenly Robin Richmond becomes a part of the story. My father implies that he's been carrying on with the organist's woman. Anyway, there's a woman somewhere in the story, a woman to fight over. There *is* a fight. On the dance floor or in the underground car park? It's unclear; but the story suddenly shifts to the car park anyway, and it's Robin Richmond punching him, and knocking him out; yet the music seems to go on playing.

Someone knocks my father out anyway, and he either gets into, or is pushed inside a car, on to the back seat. He has a lot to sleep off. The story cuts suddenly to South London, to Balham, and Ellis wakes up, not knowing where he is. The drivers of the car have brought him all the way from Blackpool, not realizing he's in the back. It's outside a lodging house, the car; the people are friendly. He eats bacon and eggs, 'looks around a bit', decides he 'likes the look of the place', borrows ten pounds, goes back North to 'collect a few things', coming back down again to the city in which he was to pass the next forty years of his life. He emphasized 'the few things': the phrase meant more than was apparent: one day, secrets might be revealed.

It's a good story, an allegory I think, that covers a plainer tale. Something had gone wrong, he was scared, he had to get out of town. Fifteen years after the telling, long after his death, looking at the suddenly revealed photograph on the bedroom mantelpiece, I found out what it was he'd left behind.

*

Underneath the Hammersmith flat, the flat we left in the

early summer of 1951, was a cellar. It was part of the huge gothic building next door where he worked. It ran underneath our first-floor flat too, but to reach it you had to go down the stairs and out into the street first. Down here, my father kept his tools, and sometime during the year before we moved he started to make me a dolls' house. My mother took me down there to show me work in progress, the bare toy rafters and the little roll of tiled wallpaper for the roof. My father was surprised to see us, and in retrospect it is very odd that we should have made this descent, for later on, his not understanding the conventions of emotional life, like keeping surprises a secret – or preparing any sort of surprise, giving any sort of present – was to be one of the many items on my mother's check-list of his failures.

My mother leant back against a workbench, her hands on its edge behind her. It tipped her body forward, just a little. She leant back; she laughed, she smiled. Ellis stood under the spot of light, a plane in his hand, a smile: a charmer charmed. Years later it becomes quite clear that this was the place where my mother set in motion my father's second seduction. She'd tried with having me, and it hadn't worked. Now, a second and final attempt. By the time he took me to the bluebell wood, my sister was born, and our life was set on its sad course. The scene of seduction remained a mystery for a very long time, an area of puzzlement that failed to illuminate, like the light absorbing the darkness over the workbench. When I consciously thought about the mysteries of their relationship, I used in fact a highly literary set of devices.

My intensest reading of the fairy-tales was during the summer of my seventh year. The feeling of nostalgia and regret for how things actually are was made that June as Gerda in 'The Snow Queen' looked for Kay along the river banks that were eventually to lead to the queen's frozen palace, and she came to the place where the old woman, the witch, made all the rose trees sink into the dark ground so that Gerda would stay with her, not be reminded by the flowers of Kay, for whom she is searching.

Out the back, outside the room where the child reads the book, there grew a dark red rose with an ecstatic smell. The South London back gardens pressed up against the open window like a sadness in the dusk, and I lay on my bed, and read, and imagined what it was they were doing downstairs. The wireless was playing and I saw this picture: they both sat naked under the whitewood kitchen table, their legs crossed so that you couldn't really see what lay between. Each had a knife, sharp-edged with a broad yet pointed blade, and what they did with the knife, what the grown-ups did, was cut each other, making thin surface wounds like lines drawn with a sharp red pencil, from which the blood poured. In the book the Little Robber Girl whom Gerda has encountered on her journey north

> pulled out a long knife from a crevice in the wall and drew it across the reindeer's neck; the poor animal kicked with its legs, and the Robber Girl laughed and then pulled Gerda into bed with her. 'Do you take the knife to bed with you?' asked Gerda, looking some-what scared at it. 'I always sleep with a knife,' said the Little Robber Girl. 'One never knows what may happen.'

Downstairs I thought, the thin blood falls in sheets from my mother's breasts; she was the most cut, but I knew it was she who did the cutting. I couldn't always see the knife in my father's hand.

In the same book, another girl, another woman – the Little Mermaid – longs to enter the world above the sea from which she is excluded by being what she is: 'More and more she came to love human beings, more and more she wished to be among them. Their world she thought, was far larger than hers.' It is love that will help her enter this world, desire for the prince whom she watches obsessively, as she swims round his ship, night after night. To enter this world of adult sexuality, to gain two legs instead of a fish's tail, she strikes a bargain with the Sea Witch: she must feel every step as if walking on the edge of knives, and her tongue must be cut out. In pain, dumb and silenced, she makes her sacrifice in vain, for the prince does not love her back; and when the day of his marriage to a mortal dawns, the Little Mermaid must die. Her sisters of the sea offer her the chance of life: by killing the prince and having his warm blood fall on her feet, her legs will join together again, into a fish's tail. But instead she sacrifices herself, flings away the knife, and is dissolved into the foam on the waves.

The fairy-tales always tell the stories that we do not yet know. Often, a few years later, I would long for my mother to get rid of my father, expel him, kill him, make him no more, so that we could lead a proper life. And what I know with hindsight about that summer of the fairy-tales, is that a new drama was in process of enactment. The removal of my father by the birth of my sister (an old, conventional story, every eldest daughter's tale) was being formalized by my mother's warfare against him, a warfare that always stopped short of banishment; and I was to end up ten, indeed twenty years later, believing that my identification was entirely with her, that whilst hating her, I was her; and there was no escape.

The Little Mermaid was not my mother sacrificing herself for a beautiful prince: I knew her sacrifice: it was not composed of love or longing for my father, rather of a fierce resentment against the circumstances that were so indifferent to her. She turns me into the Little Mermaid a few years later, swimming round and round the ship, wondering why I was not wanted, but realizing that of course, it had to be that way: 'How could he do it,' she said, 'leave two nice little girls like you?'

*

Our household and the registrar general's socio-economic categories mask a complicated reality. Social class is defined by a father's occupation, and during my childhood we must have belonged to class III (manual). A heating engineer without any training, he did get inside boilers and mend them, but more often told other men what to do. He was, in effect, a foreman. I think that for my mother, years before in the 1930s, her relationship with him had been a step up, a kind of catch for the weaver's daughter. His parents had once kept a corner sweet shop, and my mother told me when I was about eleven that they'd briefly had a pony and cart before losing it, and the business. She spoke of this vehicle, in which she'd never ridden, with a diffident pride: the little nod of pleased possession. But the pleasure had to be ambiguous now: she was already long engaged in revealing my father's meanness, vulgarity and lack of ambition. When he married in 1926 he gave his trade as traveller for a firm of mill-part manufacturers in York. There's a photograph that looks as if it were taken about this time showing a woollen mill decorated for Christmas, the girls turned towards the camera, their looms still, and standing amongst them one man, my father in a collar and tie, a visitor from the mobile world outside.

If we'd lived within my father's earning power, been uncomplicatedly his children, two meals a day round the kitchen table, parents sharing a bed (and the *car*; in all those years my mother was never driven anywhere in the firm's car) then our household would actually have represented, and represented to its children, the unambiguous position of the upper working class. But it was my mother who defined our class position, and the emotional configurations that follow on such an assessment. What is more, until we were in our thirties, my sister and I continued to believe that she bore the major burden of supporting us. As children we believed that without her we'd go hungry, and the knowledge of how little we cost came very late indeed.

He had nothing to give her in exchange for herself, not even the name that the statute books would allow him to bestow on her (and probably wouldn't have given it to her had he been able). The house was rented, the weekly seven pounds was payment for us, not a gift to her. She made us out of her own desire, her own ambition, and everything that came her way in the household was a by-product of our presence and her creation of our presence. We were an insurance, a roof over her head, a minimum income. We were her way of both having him and repudiating him. We were the cake that she both had and ate, before he left (though he never really left), and after.

In 1958 I passed the eleven-plus, and in August of that year the uniform I needed for grammar school was the subject of angry debate. He'd been approached for money for the gaberdine mac, the tunic, the shoes, and he had handed some over, but not a lot. The uniform must have been a strain on the seven pounds. The issue, this Saturday afternoon, is the blouses that I will have to wear. I'm wearing a new one anyway, one from Marks & Spencer with blue embroidery round the collar, as I approach him at my mother's persuasion and drag his attention away from the form on telly. He asks why I can't wear the one I've got on. I'm profoundly irritated, outraged at his stupidity; they don't allow it, I say: it's a *rule*.

He did know some rules, but he didn't embody them: they were framed by some distant authority outside himself. For instance: I had become very timid in the years after 1951, often frightened of falling down, of appearing a fool. I disgraced him that summer in the public eye, sitting at the top of the slide on the Common, a queue of impatient children behind me, frozen with fear, quite unable to let go of the sides and slide down. In disgrace I turned round, made my shameful way down the steps again, the children parting in front of me and my father apologizing to the adults with them. He took me home and complained to my mother: there's something wrong with her, a child of five ought not to be frightened; a child of five ought to be able to slide.

He waited for me on the doorstep one time about a year later after he'd sent me down the road for a paper, because a neighbour watching me had said I was walking funny, looked flat-footed. I had my wellingtons on the wrong feet, it turned out. He knew the social prescriptions that said we ought to be alright, have *nothing wrong* with us – to be able to read, to walk straight – and that he was judged by our performance too.

In the mid-fifties he started to live in the attic, treated the place like a hotel. The firm put a telephone in the house, about 1956, so that he could deal with emergencies about burst boilers in the middle of the night. He came home at six o'clock, collected phone messages, made a mug of tea, washed, went out to his other life. Whilst we were children he always came back, sometimes before midnight. In the attic he read the *Evening Standard*, smoked a cigarette before he went to sleep. I interpret this nightly return as an expression of the ambivalent responsibility that lay in the seven pounds handed over on Friday, as a failure either to desert us or to change the situation he'd put us in: a man serving out his time, the maintenance payments as much a matter of obligation as those imposed in a bastardy order issued by a court of law. My sister says he came back because he didn't want to commit himself anywhere. He was a man of benevolent irresponsibility.

She wouldn't feed him, after about 1958, but he was allowed tea. Every morning in a red tartan dressing-gown he made his own. She must have bought the tea (that we were never permitted to drink) out of the seven pounds. Tea was tea and milk was milk (except for a brief flirtation with goats' milk, at which all the worms turned) but she had some choice over sugar, and refused to buy white poison. There was a long time, about 1960, when he complained every morning about the grittiness and how it made the tea taste. Later, I think he bought his own packets of Tate & Lyle.

We still had lodgers in the 1960s, not the glamorous turn-over of the theatrical years, but sad, long-term men. My father met the newly arrived watch-mender on the stairs and said 'Hello, I'm the other lodger,' and the watch-mender believed him for days. This incident was remembered, given the status of a joke (our only family joke), an explanatory device, for my father to recall ten years later in the pub, for me and my sister to remember and laugh over after my mother's funeral. Curtailment of activity and exclusion from particular rooms of the house was a rule that my mother put into effect for all those men who handed over payment to her. The watch-mender wasn't allowed to use the bath – she said he was too dirty. This stricture didn't apply, however, to the Indian student who occupied the room before him. My mother explained that Hindus had to wash in running water and that they found us dirty. He had the charm of the exotic for her: anything foreign, over which she could show a classy tolerance, was a route away from her social situation. Later, she was to call herself a Powellite.

On Saturday afternoon the front room became briefly my father's territory. Racing on the telly, bets over the phone to the bookie, mugs of tea, whisky later on. He cleared the room after the football results and when he'd checked his coupon. This usage, I now understand, was his right within the treaty negotiated somehow with my mother. I could have read those rights in other actions, in the way, for instance, if he came home early on a weekday night and found us still in the front room, he'd switch off the lights, and fire and television, and leave us in the dark as he went upstairs to the attic; and in the permanently dismantled electric fire in my room, so that I could only ever burn one bar.

*

My father used to say: 'She's a wonderful woman, your mother,' or sometimes 'She's a bloody wonderful mother, Edna is.' When? When I asked him, on her instructions, for something. There was a long campaign, about 1961, to get him to buy a unit to replace the deep porcelain sink in the scullery (he didn't); pressure a few years later to get him to buy a house, and then to make a will. When I hear of passive resistance, I think of my father. All pleadings were now made through me. I would feel the justice of my mother's cause, raise the matter, usually Saturday lunch times after he got home from work, and before the racing started, plead the case, argue that she worked so hard. He never capitulated; listened; then: 'She's a bloody marvellous mother, your mother.' I can never read this deadly rejoinder, never, however many times I rehearse it, *hear* what it was he was saying. In interpretation it falls this way, then that; I don't know what he meant. It was a statement beyond irony (though it was ironic, in a way I couldn't and wasn't expected to understand: information withheld). He meant it in some way, revealed that he had surrendered to her interpretation of events, was playing the role assigned to him. Sometimes drink was mentioned: 'She doesn't drink, your mother.' I think the stories of maternal neglect brought from pre-War Lancashire expressed a reality that both of them knew about. Much later, he was genuinely shocked when, at twenty-seven, I wrote to my mother and said that I didn't want to see her for a while because she upset me so much. He said then that she'd been a good mother; but he'd forgotten the unassailable irony of fifteen years before.

There were fits and starts in their relationship, so dramatically altered at Christmas 1954. They got together again, the attic temporarily abandoned, about 1961. There were meals together; I remember weeping at Sunday dinner time into a bowl of tinned fruit, the tinned food itself a sure sign that some truce was being enacted. But it didn't last. Once, a dreadful time, the other life invading ours ('There's that woman on the phone again;' 'Why tell me?' 'Who else is there to tell?'), I packed all his things in the suitcases, and put them in the hall. I wanted him to go, for *something to happen*, something to change. I saw the future – work, the journey home, the quick meal, television, tiredness, my mother's life – stretching ahead for ever, like the long streets of South London houses; no end ever to be seen. But he didn't go. Nothing changed.

I still see him in the street, seven years after his death, a man of his generation, an old man at a bus-stop, his clothes hanging in folds; a way of walking. I shall never see my mother in the street in this way; she, myself, walks my dreams.

When he died I spent days foolishly hoping that there would be something for me. I desperately wanted him to give me something. The woman he'd been living with handed over two bottles of elderberry wine that they'd made together out of fruit gathered from the side of the ring road where her flat was. I drank one of them and it gave me the worst hangover of my life.

He left us without anything, never gave us a thing. In the fairy-stories the daughters love their fathers because they are mighty princes, great rulers, and because such absolute power seduces. The modern psychoanalytic myths posit the same plot, old tales are made manifest: secret longings, doors closing along the corridors of the bourgeois household. But daddy, you never knew me like this; you didn't really care, or weren't allowed to care, it comes to the same thing in the end. You shouldn't have left us there, you should have taken me with you. You left me alone; you never laid a hand on me: the iron didn't enter into the soul. You never gave me anything: the lineaments of an unused freedom.

Part three

Interpretations

When a child first becomes conscious of himself, the way of life of his parents and companions will appear both natural and inevitable, but as he grows older and gains some knowledge, however incomplete, of other forms of existence, so he will begin to comprehend the peculiarity of his situation.

(David Vincent, *Bread, Knowledge and Freedom: A Study of Nineteenth Century Working Class Autobiography*, p. 90)

Living Outside the Law

Every time a mother threatens her children with 'I'll
tell your father . . .' though she has in mind a real
person and a real situation . . . it is to the symbolic
father behind the actual father that her words refer.
The dead father of the law . . . is there, however
weak or absent his real representative may be,
however dominant the mother, however 'matriar-
chal' the particular situation . . .

    (Juliet Mitchell, *Psychoanalysis and Feminism*)[1]

On Saturday morning I had to stop in. I played with
my Tiny Tears and my pram. Then my brother
came in to jump on his bed, so he did. Soon we came
down and my mum went up to make the beds.
When she came down she was angry. I asked her
why and she said, You just wait till your father gets
home and then you'll have something to jump
about, and I said What's wrong? And she said to
me, Your brother has broken a leg off his bed. But
she did not tell my dad.

    (Girl, 8 years old, diary entry, 1976)[2]

My parents were immigrants. Strangers to a metropolis
during a great depression, they left a northern country,
impossible stories left behind them: a wife and child abandoned. In London they created a new set of impossibilities,
the matter of terrible secrets. All family secrets isolate those
who share them. Secrets which derive from the play of
fantasy, from rivalry, hatred and desire may be unconsciously transmitted across time and generation, achieving

the status of a myth.[3] Real secrets, real events that are
concealed by some members of a family, may be matters of
legal impropriety and thus connected to the social world
outside the household; but such secrets can also produce
myths of origin that serve both to reveal and conceal what is
actually hidden from view. The myth may at the same time,
and seemingly as part of the mechanism of concealment,
interpret the world beyond the house walls in a way that
reveals something of the social meaning of the hidden event.

Among the things that my parents left behind in the North
was a complex net of relationships and the support of kin.
In my mother's family this was a process that had anyway begun before her birth, with the emigration to
Massachusetts of her eight uncles and aunts. The known and
knowable community was already attenuated by this watery
distance when she made her own migrant's journey south.

Both my parents were only children, but it is not this
factor that explains the isolation of our childhood. We got
to know, much later than the 1950s, that there were cousins
and half-cousins littered over the deserted terrain of the mill
towns; but we met none of them. I saw my maternal
grandmother on only six occasions during her lifetime
(which ended in 1981), and my father's mother only once
before she died in 1954. No one ever visited the South
London house. The only person ever to stay in it was my
grandmother, who had looked after me in the Hammersmith flat when my mother was in hospital having my sister,
and who stayed twice again, with seven years between the
visits, in the house in Streatham Hill. One of the hardest
lessons of my young adulthood was discovering that it was
possible to invite people into a household, to have them to
stay, and that the presence of outsiders did not necessarily
mean invasion and threat. But such an anxiety did attach to
the practice, and for such a very long time, that I have
to re-read my childhood in the light of that anxiety, see
the refusal of entry to outsiders not as the normality it
was experienced as at the time, but rather as a series of

covert messages about the impropriety and illegality of our existence.

No friends of my parents came to call: my mother had no friends. My father had dozens, but we only heard about them, never met them: 'tap-room friends' she called them. Very occasionally, children from the street passed through the narrow corridor to the kitchen and the back yard. This wasn't encouraged, though: we played in general in other children's houses. If the doorbell rang when we were eating, we were not allowed to answer it. Years later I read about this reluctance to reveal the poverty of food on the table in several working-class autobiographies and thought: yes, that must have been it. I added the monotony of our diet after 1954 and the later diminution of crockery and cutlery to this ascribed sociological motivation on my mother's part, and was satisfied. But the practice represented more than that. It was a demonstration that we were in a particular way, living outside the law. Enforced isolation was due to the adults keeping their heads down, out of the geographical firing line of censure from the North, preventing possible leakage of information, the door closed against any discovery of their secrets.

They had brought with them nothing but their labour, and the capacity, forced upon them by the economic exigencies of the 1920s and 1930s, to exchange one set of skills for another, to turn their hand to whatever came along. What else was carried was only the clothing to fill a suitcase, like the contents of the tin box that went with the child from Coventry to Burnley, or the trunks in the hold on the Atlantic passage. And yet: there was a peculiar emphasis in my father's allegory of escape, told in the pub in the 1960s, when he came to the part about going back home 'to collect a few things'. What kind of thing, what kind of possession, was my mother? If he did collect her on that rapid journey it's certain that no conventional marriage bargain was enacted, that no one gave her to him, and that all she brought to the partnership was herself.

Across time and culture, women have been written of as objects of exchange among men: Freud's Dora contemplates her price in the gift of a jewel-case,[4] and in a synthesizing anthropological essay, 'The Traffic in Women', Gayle Rubin shows us women who along with 'children, shells, words, cattle, names, fish, ancestors, whales' teeth, pigs, yams, spells, dance mats ... pass from hand to hand, leaving in their tracks the ties that bind.' It is women who are transacted says Rubin, and it is men who give them and take them, across time, across cultures.[5] We do not discover from this essay what women might think and what they might come to know as they are passed along the routes of transaction. *The Making of the English Working Class* is evoked, and the specific understanding of the self as object and subject, needed to make oneself a factory worker out of being a craft worker in early nineteenth-century England is indicated.[6] But Gayle Rubin does not pursue the question raised by Thompson, that is, of the *activity* of human beings, as they are translated as objects, as gifts, hands or workers, into something else. We end up with fine insights into the minds of those who do the exchanging, but knowing next to nothing about the understanding of those who, like yams and shells, are the object of exchange.

'To enter a gift relationship as a partner, one must have something to give. If women are for men to dispose of, they are in no position to give themselves away.'[7] This is the pivotal point of the unwritten psychology that lies at the heart of Rubin's essay. It is compelling because of the silences it contains, and its silences can be evoked to tell us about cracks in the patriarchal law that the essay describes. The silences also indicate the relationship of that law to the material possession of things in the social world. Under particular social circumstances, people may come to understand that whilst they do not possess any*thing*, they possess themselves, and may possibly be able to exchange themselves for something else. Under such circumstances, there exists the specificity of a woman's situation, and the understanding of herself as an object of exchange that may arise when she has some choice over reproduction, and can use herself and her children as a traffic with the future. In its turn, the understanding that young children living in these circumstances may come to gain about themselves, as items of expenditure, investments, and as objects of exchange, needs to be taken into account as well.[8] In general then, I want to consider the usefulness of the idea of a traffic in women, bring it forward to post-Second World War Britain, where my mother exchanged herself for a future – that she anyway believed was her rightful inheritance. This transaction, which has to be seen in both political and psychological terms, is what the rest of this book is about; but for more immediate purposes it is used to suggest that the notion of patriarchal law has to be seen within the framework of ownership and possession, that its status as an interpretative device is altered when women are seen as owning something, even if it is only their labour, and the babies they produce.

My mother's decision (reconstructed from circumstantial evidence) to produce children as levers, as possibilities, must have been made in the knowledge of herself as both bargain and bargainer. It's probable that knowledge like this becomes more generalized and available to conscious reckoning in situations of geographical shift and change. Writing about the immigrant proletariat of the USA, John Berger remarks that

> unable to return home, suffering from being who they were, [they] yearned to become, or for their children to become, American. They saw no hope but to exchange themselves for the future. And though the desperation of the wager was specifically immigrant, the mechanism has become more and more typical of developed capitalism.[9]

(And surely too, those women, passed across deserts, sent through mountain passes – yams, goats, beads, shells, women – began at some point to see themselves as something they could exchange for a possible future.)

The idea of traffic and exchange, in and of the self, and of labour, applied also to my father, must apply to all those who find themselves in moments of transition and in places of escape. But he merely exchanged a past for a possible future; he did not place himself on the bargaining table as my mother did. Having the capacity to bear children, she took a gamble, exchanged a part of herself for the hope that he would marry her, bring her within the law; or to put it more generally: that a baby, a part of herself split off and made manifest, would not only insure a future but would also *be* a future.

In this case, then, she was a woman who had something to give, and her rights in her children derived not solely from the illegality of my father's position (for in one sense he legalized us, by paying for us, supporting us, staying around), but also from the choice she was able to make, specific to time and place and – relatively newly – to her class, about the disposal of her body. Her production of children and the wishes and desires that the production embodied were a manifestation of a process that has become much more widespread and certainly more discussed over the last ten years, of a bargain struck between working-class women and the state, the traffic being a baby and the bargain itself freedom, autonomy, state benefits and a council house: the means of subsistence.[10]

*

In the city where my parents found a hiding place, they produced two illegitimate children. The secret was not revealed until 1977, but as a child I worried a great deal about what seemed a particular illegality of my sister's existence. At the Sunday school to which I had so reluctantly gone along, but which soon took on the aspect of a social occasion, I found out about baptism. My sister hadn't been christened, I knew that, and I approached my mother on the topic. She told me that I had been baptized, in Hammersmith, but that the couple who stood as god-parents had disappeared: 'We lost touch with them.' She then either reminded me of, or I remembered at that point, a scene of four years before, a crowded pavement outside a church just off Hammersmith Broadway, the people gathered there to watch a double wedding, the event made newsworthy by one of the brides, in the post-War clothing shortage, having sewn her dress out of a kind of plastic raincoat material, pale green and shiny with embossed flowers, fitting closely over her hip and curved like a fish's tail. That was the church you were christened in, she said; and there's no telling now whether she said it first that summer day in 1950 as we stood watching the wedding from the pavement, or now, four years later, as I question her agitatedly in the scullery about my sister's status in the light of eternity.

They had said at Sunday school that the unbaptized couldn't enter heaven. I had consulted the teacher of my group, and she'd told me that people didn't have to be babies to be christened. I told my mother this, and tried to get her to arrange a ceremony for my sister. Then, in the face of evasion, the idea faded. It was this revealed difference between me and my sister, though, that permitted my growing recognition that we represented different stages of endeavour to my mother, that my sister was a disappointment in the way that I wasn't. It was a genuine shock *not* to find a baptismal certificate with my name on it after her death, among all the papers stuffed into drawers and old handbags, a shock to discover that I wasn't the privileged elder daughter after all. I remembered then how Sunday school had strangely stopped when confirmation classes had begun and I told her that I would need to take the certificate to church some time. She had, they both had, what they thought were terrible secrets to keep. Unknowing, with dissimulation, I learned of their existence without being able to see what those secrets actually were.

It was half-remembered incidents like these, interpreted

by limited and misleading information, that much later provided a quite different understanding of being outside the law. A sense of dislocation can provide a sharp critical faculty in a child.[11] I stood outside, watching, could bring forward incidents of my childhood to question all the official interpretative devices that I encountered. The scene in the bluebell wood with my father, the eruption of the angry keeper, was re-imagined when I was set to read *Totem and Taboo* and *Moses and Monotheism* at twenty. It was a way of thinking about the oedipal account, its relation to the myth of the primal act of patricide, the incest taboo and the whole generalized account of human culture built around the position and role of the father. It was a way of wondering about how the myth works when a father is rendered vulnerable by social relations, when a position in a household is not supported by recognition of social status and power outside it. That scene was a way of saying: no: it wasn't like that; he wasn't important; he didn't matter.

The accidents of history and circumstance allowed a child a sharp and watchful intelligence: there is something that puzzles in the scenes watched from the pavement. The legal impropriety of my existence, and the sudden covert revelations of this impropriety permitted sightings of fractures within the system we inhabit, which is variously called patriarchy, or a sex-gender system, or the law. There are these two ways of understanding the law, the space between two meanings, and their meeting place.

*

I am irresistibly drawn to accounts that display the disjuncture between systems of authority in class societies that I witnessed as a child. Working-class autobiography frequently presents, as a moment of narrative revelation, a child's surprise at the humility of a domestic tyrant witnessed at his work-place, out in the world.[12] As a concomitant to such moments of revelation, the authority of the working-class father within the household has been established as a tenet of cultural criticism, with Richard Hoggart, for instance, remarking in 1957 that 'the point of departure for an understanding of the position of the working class father in his home, is that he is the boss there, the "master in his own house".'[13]

Beyond the point of initial surprise, none of the literature deals with what happens to children when they come to witness the fracture between social and domestic power, as did John Pearman's children in 1867. John Pearman was a policeman – and a radical, a republican, a socialist – who was stationed at Eton between 1864 and 1881.

He wrote an account of his life and political development in 1881/2, and in his *Memoir* describes at great length a dramatic confrontation, witnessed by his children, between his meaning as a father and his place in a system of class relations.[14] Ordered out of town by the master of Eton in 1867 because several of his youngest children had scarlet fever, and after a desperate search for a conveyance for his highly infectious family, he stops at the side of the road when the sickest of the children starts to vomit.

> A Gentalman came up on Horseback and said do you know whats the matter with that Boy. I did not answer him as the Boy was Vomiting he said he as the Scarlet Fever I replied I know that. He then looked into the Fly and said (Inspector I had my uniform on) they have all got the fever were are you taken them to I replied unto Winkfield he said no that you shan't . . . he said what is your name I am the Doctor of Winkfield and must know.

John Pearman was defiant on this occasion (in the way I find it difficult to remember my father being in the woods), showed the doctor the paper for his family's removal. They then waited by the side of the road whilst the doctor rode back to Eton to talk to the Master of the college. He came back 'in a better temper', and the family went on their way. But it's not the outcome that signifies. It's the children watching the confrontation from the carriage that we should look at, watch their watching the disjuncture between two systems of authority: their father a man in uniform (yet thrown out of town); the gentleman on the horse.

The conventions of working-class autobiography, the positioning of an articulated solidarity (of family and friendship, of street and factory) against an external authority of school, the Guardians, the Assistance Board, or the police, make it difficult to represent this dislocation of class and economic relations within the household.[15] It is also much more difficult for women to make a representation of such dislocation, for the conventions of the literary form, which has been largely developed by men, demand that the mother be embraced as 'the best woman who ever lived' if the father is in any way exposed or condemned.[16] Some women, however, have managed to represent the dislocation in a convoluted way, Kathleen Woodward in *Jipping Street* for instance, who did not write autobiography but rather a psychic reconstruction of childhood in London at the turn of the century, an account in which she can both realize and resent her mother's strength. In *Jipping Street* she makes her father an invalid, an absence coughing behind closed doors.[17] Kathleen Dayus's account of working-class childhood in Birmingham during the same period, *Her People*, is remarkable for the ease with which she can show sympathy for a father whose life, she knows perfectly well as a child, is much easier than her mother's. Her furtive resentment of her mother and her nervous revulsion from her body tell a story that lies outside the literary framework of working-class autobiography.[18] The myths need recasting to become interpretative devices for such material.

In my own account, the official psychoanalytic myths ignore the social powerlessness that the scene in the bluebell wood reveals, speak to other matters: to the illegal picking of the flowers, the vulnerability of their white roots. But the point of the symbolic scene lies at the moment of its use, not in historical time; its point is perhaps the place where it enables me to watch John Pearman's children watch the play of class relations on the road to Winkfield in 1867, to understand that both scenes show men whose meaning for their children is altered and restrained by the position they occupy in a class society.

The official myths must place us in this extreme difficulty, for they have become more than the framework of a therapeutic discipline – that of psychoanalysis – they have become the stuff of our 'cultural psychology', the system of everyday metaphors by which we see ourselves and our past.[19] The difficulty is compounded by the fact that the evidence compiled within the psychoanalytic enterprise has been used to analyse the workings of a social system within historical time, that is, to outline the mechanisms of patriarchy in the capitalist West of the last two hundred years, and the way women get to be the way they are, living under this dual system. So, whilst the historical boundaries of psychoanalysis are recognized (in strictly historical terms it can't tell us about much more than the vicissitudes of living in a particular section of Viennese society in the late nineteenth century), the evidence itself is used to explore the experience of women from many different class, cultural and geographical backgrounds in the nineteenth and twentieth centuries.

There is a common objection to Freud's rewriting of the myth of Oedipus, and the accounts of female sexuality that both feed his rewriting and derive from it, in the cultural specificity of late nineteenth- and early twentieth-century Vienna. In both historical and anthropological terms, though, this accident of milieu was useful, because it enabled Freud to examine 'the "eternal" structures of patriarchy in what for us is their most essential particularity: the bourgeois, patriarchal family'.[20] Yet even seen in this way, the official myths continue to present difficulties, and much of this difficulty is to do with what happens when the stuff of one discipline, one mode of thought, is used as evidence within another. The original psychoanalytic corpus is evidentially bound, which matters not at all to the operation of psychoanalytic theory itself; but when the material that makes up the theory is used for historical or anthropological purposes, the absence of so large a number of people from its evidential base has seemed to demand immediate adjustment. Various sociological notions have been attached to it, in order to make it represent more fully the social system that it is being used to describe.

The usual device for this adjustment, for the rapid insertion of the working class into the theory, has been the construction of various models of imposition and transmission, the commonest being the assertion that within recent history the model of the bourgeois family has been imposed upon working-class households, and that the idea and image of this family has become our way of seeing and understanding all families.[21] This imposition, according to one authority, is 'one of the unwritten aspects of the political success of bourgeois democracy'.[22] There are, however, few historical accounts of such imposition and transmission of ideas, and the historical process by which people, in both assessing and using the ideas presented to them, actually resist them, is scarcely considered. Large-scale sociological assertions about the transmission of family patterns and the psychic patterns they give rise to, from one class to another, allow the original subjects of psychoanalytic case-study an active role in the production of historical evidence, whilst the much larger number of people to whom it is suggested these understandings are passed on, are seen simply as the passive objects of transmission.[23]

It is the social imbalance of evidence within the psychoanalytic corpus, *when that corpus comes to be used historically*, that prevents our seeing the cracks in the system where John Pearman's children watch from the carriage window on the road to Winkfield, and where I watch the parkkeeper snatch the bluebells from my father's hand. The corpus draws its images from the social world (it could scarcely do otherwise); it is made out of metaphors that look as if they describe nothing at all, but rather simply *are* the way the world is: a jewel-case, a pair of pearl ear-rings, a nursemaid, a household ordered this way, now that, a tree outside the nursery window. The quiet order of imagery, the complacency with which objects are presented in the narrative of case-study, operate in something of the manner of the fairy-tale, where we do not doubt that the princess, or the bag of silver, or the golden goose are desirable, because the people in the story, by their wanting, demonstrate that they are so.[24] This story, the psychoanalytic story, could not use the stuff of the world outside the gate in this way: streets, food, work, dirt, can only be used to dispel the complacency of the imagery. The narrative holds within itself sets of images that represent the social divisions of a culture, and only with extreme difficulty can it be used to present images of a world that lies outside the framework of its evidential base.

We can see this imbalance in other terms, in the disjuncture that lies in the telling, in a narrative account that presents its constituents as neutral, but that actually draws on socially specific images for its construction, detailing the bourgeois household where doors shut along the corridor, hiding secrets that the actors in the drama have themselves created. It operates like the fairy-tales which say to children: here are some kings and queens, a lost kingdom: use these figures to think about what you know. That children do use these items of romance, and that the psychoanalytic framework can be used across the barriers of class in spite of the actual and historical differences between an imposed ideology of the family and working-class family arrangements, is to do with the desire to be part of a story, even if it is someone else's.

*

The pivotal point of this framework, when it is used in this explanatory and historical way, is the patriarch, who is seen to be present even in his absence:

> A patriarchal society bequeaths its structure to all of us
> (with important variations according to the material
> conditions of class and race) gives us . . . the cultural
> air we breathe . . . whether or not the actual father
> is there does not affect the perpetration of the
> patriarchal culture within the psychology of the in-
> dividual; present or absent 'the father' has his place.
> His actual absence may cause confusion, or on
> another level, relief, but the only difference it makes
> is within the patriarchal assumption of his presence.
> In our culture he is just as present in his absence.[25]

The term patriarchy has been used to make many different analyses of women's oppression, of the sets of rules and
laws that delineate such oppression, and of the understanding of these rules and laws that children have to acquire in
order to become members of a society.[26] In 'The Traffic in
Women' Gayle Rubin has argued that 'patriarchy' is a
highly specific term that ought only to be used of the social
situation that was originally described by it: nomadic
herdspeople organized around the rights and privileges of
a father. She suggests as a substitute the notion of 'a
sex-gender system', which implies a multifoliate variety of
sexual organization and women's oppression, but which
whilst acknowledging that all societies have organized and
will organize human sexuality in some way or other, man-
ages to avoid the historical pessimism of the idea of
patriarchy.[27]

The argument is impeccable, but it does seem necessary to
keep the term 'patriarchy' when dealing in social or historical terms, because historical analysis has to take into
account popular and contemporary formulations of theoretical notions. Juliet Mitchell complains that all the feminist
accounts she has so far read misrepresent patriarchy, de-
fining it as a social system that embodies the power of men in
general, whilst in fact 'it is quite specifically the importance
of the *father* that *patriarchy* considers'.[28] But if the actual
father is considered, then difficult questions are raised. If the

system of patriarchal law can be learned and absorbed without the active presence of a father and if 'the father . . . is just as present in his absence', then suddenly psychoanalytic theory may seem divested of psychology, suddenly innocent of a theory of *learning* in young children. The absence of a father as an imparter of patriarchal law must either posit a child's learning of it later than seems psychologically likely, must elevate the streets, schools, the processes of socialization, and books to the status of the father, or must substitute a mother who teaches his lessons, passively and simply, a mere agent of the law.

None of these objections, though, reaches the point of denying that we do indeed learn about fathers and what fathers mean through their absence and their failures as well as through their presence, and the social power that the presence of some of them may represent. It was by such failures that my mother was able to reveal to me the particular workings of a system that regulated the relations between men and women. What is a distinction though, and one that offers some hope, is the difference between learning of this system from a father's display of its social basis, and learning of it from a relatively unimportant and powerless man, who cannot present the case for patriarchy embodied in his own person.

Within accounts of the reproduction of patriarchy, the oedipal crisis has been re-read, removed from the original psychoanalytic corpus, and has been used to describe the process of acculturation, the place where a society enters a child, and a child learns the laws of a society: 'to date, the father stands in the position of the third term that *must* break the asocial dyadic unit of mother and child . . .'[29] If this term 'will always need to be represented by something or someone', then my variation of this account according to the material conditions of class – my story, the story I've told – can only be used to present disruptive evidence. In the household I grew up in (in many households of the recent past) the relationship between mother and baby was power-

fully conceived and framed in *social* terms, because the
mother belonged to a social world and the production of the
baby had social meaning. Owning some*thing*, not much,
only a pair of hands and a reproductive capacity, women
have conceived of and conceived babies as a piece of fortune, a future worker, another pair of hands; as a bloody
parcel split off from another's body, a hoped-for death with
an insurance policy to cash in; a means of escape, a contract
with the state.[30]

What broke the relationship between mother and child in
my household was indeed a representative of the law – many
representatives: a health visitor, an angry forest-keeper –
who demonstrated to us all the hierarchies of our illegality,
the impropriety of our existence, our marginality within the
social system they represented. It was not my father who
acted as the agent of the law, for he too was outside it.

There is scattered evidence from the recent history of
industrialized Britain that some children do possess a generalized apprehension that it is women who dictate the immediate terms of life. The children's story that I edited in
The Tidy House was dictated by the understanding of three
eight-year-old working-class girls, that it was their mothers
who had made a dodgy investment in having them, but who
nevertheless had *done* it, that is, it was their mothers who
had turned out the lights, made the sexual advances, had the
babies.[31] Unknowingly at the time, I interpreted their text in
the light of the seduction scene in the cellar – my father's
seduction in the basement in Hammersmith in 1950 – that I
had not yet recalled to mind. But the children's story, which
in many places is a direct representation of the social world
they knew, allows it to be used as social and psychological
evidence about that world, without any such interpretation.

Children whose fathers do not represent the lineaments of
patriarchy must learn from them about social power in
general, and the general ordering of social and economic
life. They must learn about men making circumstances and
women remaking them, about men earning more money

than women, about men being meant to keep their children, but women doing it, in fact; about how a social world is set up. Had I, at nearly nine, possessed the sharp social vision of Carla (one of the three children who wrote *The Tidy House*) then I might have been able to represent the household circumstances I knew about in this way:

> Jack, Jack, got the sack
>
> 'Oh Jack, go to work please
> to get some money for the children.'
> 'Oh all right.'
> 'Bye.'
>
> Jack came back soon, at half past two.
> Jack got the sack.
>
> 'Jack, you've got the sack.'
> 'I've got the sack.'
> 'What are we going to do now?'
> 'Don't ask me.'
>
> Jack went to every place he could think of.
> He got back home at five o'clock.
>
> 'I can't get a job now.'
>
> Jeannie his wife said,
> 'I don't care. Just get a job, Jack.
> We'll starve to death.'
>
> They had a row, and Jeannie left Jack.
> The girls came too.
>
> Oh how sad Jeannie was.
>
> She got a job as a barmaid.
> It was good money at twenty pounds a week.
> Jeannie bought Lindie a bike to ride
> and Melissa a doll and their friend Lisa a dog.
> They were happy for ever after.[32]

The presence of Carla's father did not directly represent a system of social authority, because she knew him as a man who was subject to the fluctuations of a wider economic system, knew her mother as the manager of a household, and as the ultimate financial supporter of her children. My own father was, as much as the rest of us, living outside the law; its rules were not of his making, and when on the few occasions he transmitted them to us, he was an agent of some distant ruling, not its representative. The economic system of our household, and the relationships it dictated between mother and child, meant that he could not represent for us the economic face of a wider social system. My mother, neither taken nor given in marriage, was to some extent both the subject and object of her own exchange, and analyses of patriarchal systems assume propertyless women as subjects.

But I did not understand these things at the time, in the way that Carla understood them in order to represent them in her writing. By nine I had stopped seeing; could dimly make out the fairy-stories though, that told me about the Snow Queen's icy power, the knife in my mother's hand, and the thin red lines of blood drawn across her breasts: displaying to my imagination the mutilation involved in feeding and keeping us.

Reproduction and Refusal

On one occasion my mother, fresh from drawing
her money, bought herself a small treat, something
which must have been a reminder of earlier
pleasures – a slice or two of boiled ham or a few
shrimps. We watched her like sparrows and be-
sieged her all through tea time until she shocked us
by bursting out in real rage. There was no com-
pensation; she did not want to give us this, and there
could be no easy generosity in the giving. We got
some, though we sensed that we had stumbled into
something bigger than us.
(Richard Hoggart, *The Uses of Literacy*)[1]

One can hardly tell women that washing up sauce-
pans is their divine mission, [so] they are told that
bringing up children is their divine mission. But the
way things are in this world, bringing up children
has a great deal in common with washing up sauce-
pans.
(Alice Schwarzer, *Simone de Beauvoir Today*)[2]

There is a substantial literature that deals with women's
mothering, the wish in women for a child, and the creation,
reproduction and maintenance of that wish in little girls.
This literature, which includes reformulation and expan-
sion of psychoanalytic accounts written at the end of the last
century, the accounts themselves, and modern sociological
descriptions of mothering, has colluded for the main part
with social necessity, that is, with the fact that women

are usually expected by others to want and to have children.

A more fundamental social necessity than this expectation is the fact that until recently there have been few ways in which women could, either socially or physiologically, refuse motherhood. Some mothers, though, have refused mothering, and some women have not become mothers in the first place, even though their ways of avoiding motherhood have been extremely limited and limiting (by remaining celibate for example). It is part of the purpose of this chapter to suggest what the refusal of a baby or a child is actually a refusal *of*. Some women of the recent past have attempted not to reproduce themselves (even though some of them have been mothers); have refused to behave according to the official 'rules' of good mothering.[3] The argument for this assertion rests on necessarily fragmentary evidence, on evidence that has not been reckoned within the central explanatory devices of our culture, particularly the devices of psychology and psychoanalysis. Fragmentary evidence cannot provide a coherent or unified psychological statement, but it can help begin to make a history. What statement is made has to remain within the realms of the social, because the social is the term in which it deals: refusal to reproduce oneself is a refusal to perpetrate what one is, that is, the way one understands oneself to be in the social world.

It is to marginal and secret stories that we have to look for any disturbance of the huge and bland assumption that the wish for a child largely structures femininity; and that modern feminism sees the reproduction of the wish as a *problem* makes it no less of an assumption that the wish is consistently present in all women, in all places and times. Hannah Cullwick, the Victorian housemaid who sustained a secret and sexually odd relationship with the upper-middle-class Arthur Munby for half a century probably escaped having a child because the relationship remained unconsummated. In 1872 she wrote of her baby nephew that

the little thing was very sweet to kiss but I was glad
that I wasnt the mother of a little family . . . for after all
however natural its very troublesome & after they
grow up generally a great anxiety.[4]

Her feelings about her lack of a child can be considered
separately from the reasons and motives that ensured their
absence. That she didn't possess the conscious wish for a
child had something to do with her feelings about reproduc-
ing herself: she did not quite consider herself to be a woman
in the way that her social world presented womanhood
to her. She was physically strong, undertook the dirtiest
and most degrading of housework (often at the behest of
Munby), felt the freedom of a servant's life, thought it
'better even I think than married life. For I never feel if I
could make up my mind to that – it's too much like being a
woman.'[5] Femininity was closely tied in her mind to the idea
of mothering – 'I never can really think I'm an aunt to 3 or
even 1 child – I never feel as if I'm a woman & to be called
Aunt, like my aunts' –[6] but her oblique recognition that she
was unable to reproduce herself because she was not a
woman was separate from the *social* reckoning embodied in
the first quotation from her journals, where she wrote of the
trouble and anxiety involved in the actual possession of
children.

This reckoning on her part connects with all the mothers
reported by Ann Oakley in *The Sociology of Housework*
who, before the myths of motherhood took hold, knew that
children were those who untidied the tidy house.[7] It connects with my own mother's often repeated warning: 'Never
have children dear; they ruin your life', and with the children's story edited in *The Tidy House*, which was an
attempt on the children's part to make sense of their own
mother's ambivalence about their presence, in conjunction
with the knowledge that they would one day be able
to produce children themselves.[8] Scattered evidence like
this says nothing about *how* the wish not to have a child
might come to be produced in a little girl, or in a grown

woman. But if offers traces of the wish's absence: evidence that needs heeding.

*

Within some areas of modern feminist thought, mother-hood has become a primary target for celebration. There is serious work on the thought processes inculcated by the practice of mothering – 'I speak now about a mother's *thought*, the intellectual capacities she develops, the judge-ments she makes, the metaphysical attitudes she assumes, the values she affirms. A mother engages in a discipline'[9] – and the most sustained attempt to understand how the wish to have a child is transmitted through the generations is provided by Nancy Chodorow in *Mothering: Psychoanalysis and the Sociology of Gender*.[10] Here, psychoanalytic insights are wedded to a highly specific sociological account of gender relations and mothering in the middle-class world of the white USA.

Chodorow's argument centres on the shared gender of mother and daughter and the difficulties mothers experience in perceiving their infant daughters as separate from them-selves. This sense of 'oneness and continuity' with her mother is what the little girl carries through her oedipal crisis, the transfer of affection from mother to father, into adult life.[11] A heterosexual relationship for a man repro-duces the ideal unity he once experienced with his mother; but for a woman, having been a child within a triangular relationship, having loved a woman first, something is experienced as missing within that same heterosexual relationship. The woman must look elsewhere for emotional gratification and love:

> Given the triangular situation and emotional asym-metry of her own parenting, a woman's relation to a man *requires* on the level of social structure, a third person, since it was originally established in a triangle ... On the level of psychic structure then, a child completes the relational triangle for a woman.[12]

Such an account says nothing about the way in which babies get to be little girls in the first place, recognizably the same as the mother who makes the act of gendered identification with them, and is silent about the relationship of baby girls and women outside the middle-class, heterosexual family of western sociology. Indeed, Nancy Chodorow is well aware of the limitations of her account, and knows that it is class and culture bound.[13] Were it not so bound, then the darker social side of the primary relationship between mothers and daughters, which in *Mothering* is presented as meaning that they will always 'feel alike in fundamental ways',[14] would have to emerge. For it is women who socialize little girls into acceptance of a restricted future, women who used to bind the feet, women who hold down the daughter for cliterodectomy, and who, in more familiar and genteel ways, fit their daughters for self-abasement. Writing of the woman who was her mother's former employer and who acted as her godmother, Hannah Cullwick noted that

> Her own name was *Anna Maria Dorothea* and she wanted mine to be the same. But my mother said it was too much out of the way for mine & all it sh'd be was Hannah & that'd be a scripture name and a plain name . . . so that's how my name came to be Hannah – as plain a name for a *servant* as could be.[15]

In spite of these absences however, Chodorow's *Mothering* is important, not just because of the arguments it presents and their lacunae, but also because it has helped formalize and give credence to a broader and more literary endeavour of recent years. There have been attempts to remake a system of myths in the light of these new attentions paid to mothering. In *Our Mothers' Daughters*, for example, Judith Arcana suggests that

> as Demeter and Persephone must be restored to each other, so must we all, daughters of the mother, come to acknowledge, with joy and satisfaction that 'every mother contains her daughter in herself, and every daughter her mother'.[16]

Adrienne Rich attempts the same task in calling 'the loss of the daughter to the mother . . . the essential female tragedy.'[17] Using a reconstruction of the mysteries of Eleusis for elaboration, she conjures up Demeter and Persephone in the same way, as figures created out of longing:

> Each daughter . . . must have longed for a mother whose love for her and whose power was so great as to undo rape and bring her back from death. And every mother must have longed for the power of Demeter, the efficacy of her anger, the reconciliation of her lost self.[18]

But a myth is not a wish, nor is it a longing that a particular state of affairs might come to pass. Used in psychoanalytic terms, to chart the progress of psychic life, a myth describes something that can be recognized as having happened in the life of an individual, a variant of which will occur in the life of each human being. A myth understood in this way is about a set of relationships and their inevitable outcome, and it needs to be generally recognized as such, in some manner. The story of Demeter and Persephone cannot be made to serve a mythic function because it is not a true story: it is not about what has happened, or what is bound to happen. It does not, in the case under discussion here, take into account refusal.

Accounts of mothering need to recognize not-mothering, and recognizing it, would have to deal in economic circumstances and the social understanding that arises out of such circumstances. I think that my own mother's half-conscious motive in producing me was the wish that my father would marry her, though I did not understand the economic terms of my existence that this motive dictated until long past my childhood. However, it is clear that many working-class children have understood these terms, quite precisely, and have developed an understanding of themselves in their light. Nineteenth-century girl children of the 1860s, for example, interviewed by parliamentary commissioners, demonstrated that they knew themselves as workers as well as children, knew precisely what they contributed to a household economy. Often, they described households operating at two levels, with women held responsible for feeding and clothing their children, even though they lived with a man, and that man was sometimes the father of the children. Many children seem to have handed their wages directly over to their mother, who was particularly important for managing a domestic economy that allowed wage-earning children to save up for clothes directly under her supervision.[19]

Nineteenth-century women and girls tried again and again to indicate the significance of clothes to social investigators who did not understand, and who did not know they did not understand what was being talked about, and who hurried the children on from their triviality. Within recent history decent clothing has been a necessity for any woman or girl child who wants to enter the social world: it's her means of entry, and there are rules that say so.[20] A Birmingham eight-year-old of the 1860s lays money aside, week after week, to pay for a bonnet and dress so that she can go to a Band of Hope Fete; the parents of child workers in the Nottingham lace industry dress their little girls in crinolines and ignore the lack of underwear beneath.[21] They are obeying rules, of social behaviour and social expectation. It's not that women and girls, getting by, finally making the skirt that takes twenty yards of cloth, were subverting patriarchy, or expressing a series of stratagems that had been hidden from history. (They were after all, only people doing a limited best with what life handed out to them: trying to have a modestly good time.) The practice reveals rather the way in which an external set of social rules might become a form by which a household operated. In its turn, this economic system of a household might provide a means to a child's understanding of herself. The primary identification with a mother figure that modern psychological accounts have presented, was elaborated – in the evidence of these nineteenth-century girls – by recognition of an economic duality. In becoming a worker like her mother, and in her precise understanding of the terms on which she was sent out to work, in her detailed knowledge of how money was got and laid out, the little girl showed an economic identification with her mother that was not shown by little boys – at least, not in the admittedly scanty evidence available from the last century.

It is historical accounts like this that may be used to reveal the social specificity of wanting and not wanting children in the first place, and wanting and not wanting them once they exist. Ambivalence has been characterized as a mental structure unique to the bourgeois family, the route by which a child purchases a parent's love in exchange for finding its own body disgusting.[22] In this particular account of the late nineteenth-century bourgeois child, the drama of ambivalence resulted in the child's being able to internalize a rule-system which was represented by its authority/love relationship with its parents. But there is another drama of ambivalence that nineteenth-century working-class childhood reveals, which is the child's recognition that whilst she is wanted, she is also resented: that it is economic and social circumstances that make a burden out of her, that make her a difficult item of expenditure.[23] The argument here is not that this ambivalence, nor the economic understanding that arises from it, are unique to working-class childhood, but rather that the circumstances of working-class life and household arrangements may make the knowledge more accessible to working-class children (particularly to girls) and make them more able to articulate this perception.

*

The theories of mothering sketched out at the beginning of this chapter – the psychological, the psychoanalytic, the sociological – exercise me. They draw, I know, on socially determined and quite recently evolved ideas about what good and bad mothering is. What they can't do (because they do derive from such a source) is provide any way of saying that my mother was, in fact, good enough, quite good enough in the four years we had together, before the world went wrong, for her and for me. The 'good enough' mother was born in the writings of the child analyst Donald Winnicott and has, in the fifteen years or so of her existence, come to be used as prescription, another component of the recipe for good mothering in the child-care manuals. But far from making prescription, Winnicott was in fact describing a historical reality. 'We must assume,' he wrote,

> that the babies of the world, past and present have
> been and are born into a human environment that is
> good enough, that is adaptive enough, that is adaptive
> enough in just the right way, appropriately to the
> baby's needs.[24]

I believe that as an infant I was handled and loved enough, looked at enough, was seen, and saw that I existed. My evidence for saying this (and it is not direct evidence) is that I was able to create in myself the wish for a child, which is the wish to see oneself reproduced and multiplied: 'As a result of good-enough early mothering, there develops a capacity to create a live child in fantasy.'[25] In the kitchen of the Hammersmith flat, behind the mangle in the corner, lived my two children, Joan and Maureen, one wearing a dress of blue gingham, the other of green. Maureen had dark hair, like the child in the back lane in Burnley, like my mother. Joan was fair, like me. I don't know what I did with them when I conjured them up, but they were there, behind the mangle all through the summer and winter of 1950–1, as my mother carried my yet-to-be born baby sister:

> the beginning of children is when they are conceived
> of. They turn up in the play of many children after the
> age of two years. It is part of the stuff of dreams and
> many occupations.[26]

To be 'good enough' is to do a great deal; or: it is a measure of how little is needed for survival. The unrevealed plot of Kathleen Woodward's *Jipping Street* concerns this contradiction. When the daughter presents her mother's power, there is a set of devices drawn from cultural criticism and the sociology of working-class family life to add this presentation to the conventional picture of 'our mam' – in Seabrook's conventional version 'Mum, the formidable and eternal Mum, virago, domestic law giver, comforter and martyr'.[27] But when Woodward recorded that

> I shall never know how much strength and resolution she gave me. She gave me courage ... I humbly acknowledge my debt to her, although I can never really know its nature or dimension[28]

she did so out of acknowledgement of her mother's coldness towards her, her violence and her ambivalence; and out of knowing it would have been better she hadn't been born. What was given, perhaps, was an area of freedom: an acknowledgement that it is *all right* not to love your mother, and that mothers may often not love you.

*

My mother went on being good enough: a certain liberality directed her behaviour; perhaps she even listened to Donald Winnicott on the wireless. Around the time of the first deception, the expulsion from the garden of my fourth year, I stood in the kitchen watching her sitting on a low stool, breast-feeding my sister. Interested, I asked if I could taste. She must have known, even by 1951, that it was classy not to be repulsed by bodies, and she said yes; easily, I remember her saying it. Later, she was to laugh with scorn at rumours of two children up the road who were made to have their bath with their knickers on, and years after that she would encourage us to walk round to the post-box with our dressing gowns on and our hair in rollers. The last was perhaps a way of using the street as an extension of a house, that she remembered from her own girlhood; but also, I think it was because the women's magazines told her that a certain physical licence, a defiance of the narrow conventions, was the provenance of people like Mrs Simpson, and the women whose nails she later manicured.

To a post-War child, reared entirely without confectionery, breast-milk tasted disgustingly sweet and warm; but I was very interested in the breasts. Such physical liberality did not mean that I got to know by observation what lay beneath my mother's or father's waist; but I was extremely knowledgeable about breasts, so much so that three years later, sent down the High Road with a neighbour's child to collect my mother's new corset, I was rigid with disapproval when she giggled and pointed nervously at a woman's naked breasts (something she'd never seen before, it's obvious now) glimpsed from behind a half-drawn curtain in the shop. I stared ahead, noncommittal and embarrassed, when she whispered that they looked like an ice-cream with a cherry on top. I knew this was not a thing to say, nor even to think; but thought of it myself.

It was with this most familiar part of my mother's body that I came to symbolize her ambivalence towards my existence. What came free could be given freely, like her milk: loving a baby costs very little. But feeding us during our later childhood was a tense struggle between giving and denial. We never went hungry, we were well nourished, but fed in the cheapest possible way. I knew this, I think, when I conjured her under the kitchen table, the thin wounds across her breasts pouring forth blood, not milk.

Other women have dreamed of their mother's body. 'Hers was the first body I ever looked at,' wrote Adrienne Rich

> to know what women were, what I was to be. I remember taking baths with her in the hot summers of early childhood, playing with her in the cool water. As a young child I thought how beautiful she was ... My father's tense, narrow body did not seize my imagination.[29]

But my father's did; or rather, it was part of the battlefield of his exile, and my separation from him. He began to drink heavily in the mid-fifties, ate badly, usually got pleurisy in the winter. He was at home in the kitchen one winter's afternoon, perhaps 1956 or 1957 (he must have been very ill: it's the only time I can recall his afternoon presence in the house on a weekday, and it must have been a holiday for us all to be in the house). He needed to have a poultice strapped over the lung where the infection lay. He was a thin man, with a very fair skin, his ribs showing through. He asked me to fix the adhesive tape to his back: he couldn't reach. I had to refuse, embarrassed both at my refusal and at his body, had to say no: my mother was in the scullery, listening, perhaps watching. To have touched him would have been the most terrible betrayal of her.

A little girl's body, its neat containment, seems much more like that of a man than it does that of a woman, especially if she does not really know what lies between his legs. His body was in some way mine, and I was removed from my own as well as his. Though I didn't feel the revulsion from my mother's body that Kathleen Dayus describes in *Her People* (indeed, my mother was an attractive woman who kept her figure, though she tended to put on weight very easily) I recognize the distance and distaste of the girl child from what has produced her, and what she might become:

> suddenly, Mum shot up out of bed. I'd never seen her move so quickly, nor look so misshapen as she did then, standing beside the bed with her calico shift all twisted up in front. I'd never seen her undressed before or without her whalebone stays . . . I never know how she got all that flabby flesh inside those stays. She looked so comical that I had to put my hand over my mouth to keep from laughing out loud.[30]

This isn't an expression of 'the obscure bodily self-hatred peculiar to women who view themselves through the eyes of men'.[31] It is a revulsion based on some obscure recognition of a difficulty, an ambivalence. My refusal of my mother's body was, I think, a recognition of the problem that my own physical presence represented to her; and at the same time it was a refusal of the inexorable nature of that difficulty, that it would *go on* like that, that I would become her, and come to reproduce the circumstances of our straitened unsatisfying life.

Part of the desire to reproduce oneself as a body, as an entity in the real world, lies in conscious memory of someone approving that body. I have no evidence from the time when my mother did enough to enable me to produce my fantasy children, Joan and Maureen; but my conscious memory of much later years is of rarely meeting with this kind of physical confirmation and approval. Perhaps the searches I made in female working-class autobiography when I was in my twenties were partly for the purposes of finding similar absences in other lives. They are easy enough to find. Hannah Cullwick recorded that she hardly remembered 'ever seeing her [mother] pet us and it was rare to see her kiss us after we got big',[32] and Kathleen Woodward was emphatic in *Jipping Street* that her mother 'had no love to give us, and thank God, she never pretended what she did not feel'.[33] Adrienne Rich has asked what happens to girl children in these circumstances:

> What of a woman who has to toil so hard for survival that no maternal energy remains at the end of the day ... The child does not discern the social system or the institution of motherhood, only a harsh voice, a dulled pair of eyes, a mother who does not hold her, does not tell her how wonderful she is.[34]

But the precise point of Cullwick's and Woodward's recording of this absence of physical affection and attention is that they noticed it at the same time as they began to assess the attitude of the social world towards them, and to find their place in it. Their exile from their mothers' attention mirrored a wider exclusion; which is why, though the stories of coldness towards daughters may be found in a wide range of literary and autobiographical sources, which are not of course, exclusively working class, the interpretation of that refusal is made differently by the child, according to the more general circumstances she finds herself in.

Excluded in this way, children do not develop self-love. It is self-love that lies at the root of the wish for a child, but self-love is difficult to reproduce. To know that, whilst one exists, one also need not have been, that things might be better if one wasn't there at all, presents all the ingredients of contradiction, the holding together of disparate information that sharpens a child's intelligence; but the integration of the self and the mirrored self, that provides the basis of sensuality, dies in the little girl, and the refusal to mother, the removal of the looking-glass, reproduces refusal.

*

There is another way of telling this story, a version of which I read when I was seven. The Little Mermaid sacrifices herself, refuses the chance of regaining her former state, of becoming a mermaid again. She refuses to plunge the knife into the heart of the prince, and have his warm blood flow over the feet that cause her so much pain; and she is dissolved into foam on the sea. A mermaid cannot possess an immortal soul, but she is told by the spirits she joins after her death that after three hundred years of striving after being good, she may attain one:

> 'After three hundred years we shall float into the kingdom of heaven.' 'We may get there earlier,' whispered one of them. 'Invisibly we float into the houses of mankind, where there are children; and for every day on which we find a good child who brings joy to his parents and deserves their love, our time of probation is shortened. The child does not know when we fly through the room, and when we then smile with joy at such a good child, then a year is taken off the three hundred; but if we see a bad and wicked child we must weep tears of sorrow, and for every tear a day is added to our time of trial!'

All children who are brought into the world for some

particular purpose will find their own guilt for not bringing happiness to those who produced them, however little they consciously understand of those purposes at the time, and however difficult it is to work out what it might be that would bring about that happiness.[35] The mirror breaks, just as the clock strikes five, and a lump of ice is lodged in the heart. Downstairs, the Little Mermaid turns the knife towards herself: the child watches, reads the book, not sure whose is the mermaid's face, her mother's or her own.

Childhoods

> 'As she had learned to read, she perused with avidity every book that came in her way. Neglected in every respect, and left to the operations of her own mind, she considered everything that came under her inspection, and learned to think ... In this manner she was left to reflect on her own feelings; and so strengthened were they by being meditated on, that her character early became singular and permanent; but she was too much the creature of impulse and the slave of compassion.'
>
> (Mary Wollstonecraft, *Mary: A Fiction*[1])

The child furnishes the landscape: books are read, images invested with her own meaning (a knife, a long journey to the North, an icy palace). People tell their stories to the child, about other places, other childhoods; or they keep their secrets; and using them both, the child adds other detail: a revolving door, a full skirt, some flowers' roots. Worked upon and reinterpreted, the landscape becomes a historical landscape; but only through continual and active reworking:

> People's responses to the historical conditions they encounter are shaped both by the point in their lives at which they encounter those conditions and by the equipment they bring with them from earlier life experiences[2]

says Tamara Hareven in *Family Time and Industrial Time*,

but children possess very little of that equipment (and some of it is second-hand, old tales from a distant country), and in the process of acquiring it, the baggage is continually reorganized and reinterpreted.

My mother was born in a cotton town, one of the ring of weaving towns – Blackburn, Burnley, Nelson and Colne – north of Manchester. My great-grandmother, arriving in Burnley in the late 1870s, came to a relatively newly established weaving centre, one marked off from an established cotton town like Blackburn by a late influx of workers from the rural districts.[3] Rural Yorkshire has been specified as the major source of immigrants to these towns,[4] but my grandmother's background in mid-Warwickshire suggests that double-staged immigration, in her case from domestic service to factory work, might still have been common at this time.

The weavers' unions in Lancashire at this time – the late nineteenth century – had what has been called, by way of contrast with the much more exclusive spinners' unions, an 'ecumenical recruitment policy',[5] which paid off for the women who made up the majority of the Weavers' Amalgamation, bringing them an increase in wages for four-loom supervision of 33 per cent in the two decades preceding 1906 (two years after my grandmother started work as a part-timer).[6] The historical and economic background to my mother's childhood must therefore be understood as one of limited and precarious affluence, in which women were responsible for bringing home a considerable proportion of a household's income.[7]

At the turn of the century, in the three major weaving towns of Blackburn, Burnley and Preston 'no less than three quarters of unmarried women worked, and about one third of the women continued working after they were married. In Burnley, as many as 38% of married women went out to work.'[8] Several historians have commented on the specificity of a social situation in which women worked at a trade in which their wages came near to equality with those of men, and in which equality could provoke 'sceptical social inquiry'.[9] The basis for the growth of the suffrage movement among the working-class women of Lancashire has been explored by Jill Liddington and Jill Norris in *One Hand Tied Behind Us*, and that exploration deals in terms of this particular culture: of women, and women and work, and pride in work.[10]

In this particular industrial and social situation, Seabrook's delineation of 'Mum, the formidable and eternal Mum, virago, domestic law giver, comforter and martyr'[11] has to be elaborated by a woman's own understanding of herself: that a good mother brought the money home as well as getting the food on the table. My own mother operated within, (or rather, as I know now, presented the facade of operating within) Seabrook's definition of 'the good mother', as one who 'managed to feed her children even when there was not enough money, who kept them warm and clean';[12] but both his and Hoggart's versions of 'our mam' are of a woman who does not work, whose

> domestic supremacy was in part her consolation for her inability to express herself outside her marriage and family; and [which] in this respect may always have been makeshift, a substitute for forbidden personal satisfactions.[13]

But for women who work, however boring and exhausting that work may be, the double vision is provided: between what there is, and what of it one lacks. In Burnley, as in the other weaving towns, this sense of disjuncture may have been sharpened by the fact that the much smaller number of male weavers took home larger wages than the women did.[14]

Another factor on the horizon of difference and expectation in a town like Burnley in the pre-First World War years, was emigration. There is a box of postcards from Fall River, Massachusetts, sent as one by one, brother and sister planned the passage of the next member of the family to leave Lancashire. None of them were ever to return: 'after 1910,' notes one historian, 'up to 1,000 old Burnleyites attended annual reunions in Fall River.'[15]

My grandmother's eight brothers and sisters wrote of hard times, difficult journeys, painful adjustments. But the postcards were about a new place, and a new set of possibilities, and I find in Tamara Hareven's *Family Time and Industrial Time*, which is a detailed description of life at the other end of the journey in this period (not in Fall River but in the huge textile plant of Amoskeag in Manchester, New Hampshire) the most revealing accounts of what migration meant to those who undertook it. Writing of immigrants to this New Hampshire town (specifically of those from a rural European background) she notes that:

> In terms of their life goals, most people in this study viewed themselves as being in a transitional stage from that farm background to an urban middle class life style. They did not identify themselves as 'working class' even though their behaviour might suggest it.[16]

For people passing through a British town like Burnley in the half century between 1880 and 1930, there were many more opportunities for self-definition as working class than there were in Fall River, Massachusetts, or in Manchester, New Hampshire. The growth of independent labour politics, the suffrage movement, and the widespread unionization of the workforce articulated such a position, even for those who were not directly involved in such organizations or movements. But I find Hareven's outline of what she calls a 'life-plan' a most insightful way of reading that series of postcards, of understanding what sense of herself a child born in 1913, within the set of industrial and family circumstances outlined above, might take with her to a different place, and a different time. My mother never identified herself as working class[17] though a sociologist would certainly have done so, and the health visitor who made her cry by telling her the house wasn't fit for a baby knew exactly who she was. And she certainly had a life-plan; but her story is about the world's indifference to it.

A life-plan 'encompasses a wide range of goals and aspirations around which an individual or family organises its life'.[18] People formulate principles of action and organize their existence in order to reach towards the goals they have set themselves. Within the sociological framework used here, people ideally reorganize and reformulate their life-plan in the light of the social reality they encounter, 'but . . . always . . . in the context of their own customs and traditions'.[19] The formulation ignores entirely the conceptual and psychological baggage that people carry with them, and the disruptions that the irrational and the unconscious make in its running. Yet as a formulation, it removes passivity from the figures in Hoggart's and Seabrook's landscape, suggests what desperations may lie behind the doors of the terraced houses.

*

I know very little about the circumstances of my mother's early years – an only child, a father who died at the Somme when she was three, a powerful and benevolent grandmother, a working mother – only the bits and pieces of the constraining history that were delivered up to me all through my childhood. My widowed grandmother married again when my mother was in her very early teens – a bad one, a flash one – and her daughter often spoke disparagingly of my grandmother's pursuit of a modestly good time: going out, dancing, drinking. 'She liked men, your grandmother,' she said to me once, bitterly; a brief and profound lesson in the impossibility of my doing any such thing. She carried a profound sense of resentment against the circumstances of her childhood. Her system of good mothering was partly a system of defiance, that she constructed out of that resentment, and by which she could demonstrate how unlike her own mother she was. The most perceptive and responsive audience for this display had to be her own children, for it was only to them that she had given the information that allowed them to see the opposite set of images in play, the darkness round the stage. (Her good mothering though, it should be noted, did not include teaching children right from wrong, on the list that contains managing, feeding and keeping children clean and warm: she told us how to stare ahead when the conductor came past your seat on the bus, in order to save paying the fare.[20]) The custom and tradition, then, which Hareven mentions as acting as the context for people's reshaping of a life-plan, can be used to express a state of mind, in this case my mother's resentment and bitterness against early childhood experiences. Her presentation of herself as a good mother shows also with what creativity people may use the stuff of cultural and social stereotype, so that it becomes not a series of labels applied from outside a situation, but a set of metaphors ready for transformation by those who are its subjects.

She grew up at a time when economic circumstances disrupted collective ideas about what an individual's life might, or ought to be, like. At the turn of the century, and up until the First World War, 'girls in working class families north of Rochdale would automatically go into the mill – usually into the weaving shed – when they left school'.[21] A recent historian of the British labour movement may define weaving as unskilled work in the terms established by the older craft unions, and by the status that derived from those terms;[22] but the culture of the weaving towns saw this transition from school to mill not just as one that would bring cash into the household, but also as the donation of a possession to an individual:

> That was the big thing they used to talk about, the cotton workers, 'You've a trade in your hands, a wonderful trade, a weaver. A trade in your hands if you learned to weave.'[23]

But by 1927, the year my mother left school, all this had changed. The industry was in severe decline, and a child brought up in a social context where a majority of women were considered to be in possession of a skill, became an unskilled worker. Dressmaking had always been one of the few alternative trades to cotton available in Burnley;[24] but the dry-cleaners where my mother found work did not serve to give her a skill, as an apprenticeship to a dressmaker might have done some years before. Later, in the 1930s, she was driven on the path of migration not only by the same sort of (though greatly intensified) difficulties that had sent her uncles and aunts over the Atlantic, but by the propulsion, too, of desire and social aspiration.

We were all of us, going as far back as the story lets us, people moving up and down railway tracks, leaving lost relationships in different places along the line. This particular impossible story ended up in London, in the late 1940s, and one of its products was my own childhood. I see my childhood as evidence that can be used. I think it's particularly useful as a way of gaining entry to ideas about childhood – what children are *for*, why to have them – that aren't written about in the official records, that is, in the textbooks of child psychology and child analysis, and in sociological descriptions of childhood. This public assertion of my childhood's usefulness stands side by side with the painful personal knowledge, I think the knowledge of all of us, all my family, going as far back as the story permits, that it would have been better that it hadn't happened that way, hadn't happened at all.

I stayed at school late once, without telling her. There was a man from the BBC there that day who came into the eleven-plus class and recorded voices, trying us out for a children's programme. He told us that anyone who wanted to be seriously considered should stay behind at four o'clock, and I did, held rigid with excitement by the idea of fame, the idea of my voice on the same wireless as the 'Eagle of the Ninth' which all last year I had run home at night to listen to.

She was waiting on the doorstep: I withered, there was nothing I could say. She'd wanted me to go down the road to fetch a bunch of watercress for tea, and I ought to have known she couldn't go, couldn't leave my sister. I fell into the dark place of her displeasure, the sinking feeling of descent. She wasn't like my grandmother, didn't go out enjoying herself; and neither should I.

In this way, you come to know that you are not quite yourself, but someone else: someone else has paid the price for you, and you have to pay it back. You grow small, and quiet, and take up very little room. You take on the burden of being good, which is the burden of the capacity to know exactly how someone else is feeling.

Becoming good in this way has been described in psychoanalytic terms by Alice Miller, who has written of the way in which

> every mother carries with her a bit of her 'unmastered past', which she unconsciously hands on to her child. Each mother can only react empathically to the extent she has become free of her own childhood.[25]

Unfree in this way, a mother may love the child as a version of herself, something through which she may live, and achieve all her lost hopes. And so, there come into existence children who are

> intelligent, alert, attentive, extremely sensitive and (because they are completely attuned to her well-being) entirely at the mother's disposal and ready for her use. Above all they are transparent, clear, reliable and easy to manipulate.[26]

They are, in fact, children who have been made good.

But a deep resentment of these manipulations developed as I grew. I particularly resented being called cold and unfeeling in my early teens ('There's that woman on the phone again.' 'Why tell me?' 'Who else is there to tell?'

You're so unfeeling, Kay.') and would shout back in real fury that it was unfair to say that, as it was she who had made me so. I see the lineaments of this resentment, and an ultimate refusal to be manipulated, that is, in a refusal to *be* my mother, in the connection of intelligence and feeling, two aspects of the individual that Alice Miller divides from each other in *The Drama of the Gifted Child*. She argues that in the circumstances she has described the child's intellectual capacities develop undisturbed, masking often, though, a damaged world of feeling, a false and despairing self.[27] Yet intellectual development can fuel feeling: reading the fairy-tales can give a child a way of seeing what is happening, and a means of analysis. Part of my rage at my mother's accusation of coldness was due to the image of Kay in 'The Snow Queen', with a lump of ice in his heart, and quite accessible to my imagination ever since I had read the story seven years before. There was a simple fear that she might be right, that there might really be that lump of ice there; but pride too, that I *had seen* this a long time ago, that I had an image, an explanatory device. It seems that once intellectual endeavour is specified, that is, once a real child in a real situation is seen making these efforts (reading books, thinking, furnishing an imagination) then it becomes impossible to separate intellectual life from emotional life.

But I think also, that once we move from the psychoanalytic to the social (which any use of these ideas outside the therapeutic framework will provide) then the content of a mother's desire has to be specified and examined. In Miller's exegesis, mothers project 'expectations, fears and plans' on to their good children.[28] Within the theory it is quite proper that their desires retain this abstraction; but in the social world, it is the social that people want – fine clothes, a house, to marry a king; and if these desires are projected on to a child, and if she comes close to the feeling that they are her own desires as well as her mother's, then that social world itself may provide her with some measure of their quality and validity, and help her to stand to one side, momentarily detached from her mother's longing. What is more, and I find this the most hopeful and interesting feature of Miller's argument, none of this is entirely dependent on a mother: a mother only needs to be just good enough to allow the child to 'acquire from other people what the mother lacks'. Miller goes on to remark that 'various investigations have shown the incredible ability that a healthy child displays in making use of the smallest affective "nourishment" (stimulation) to be found in the surroundings'. This argument will be returned to in the next chapter.[29]

I was made good within specific class and social circumstances: to know how my mother felt meant acquaintance with all the ghostly army of good women, scrubbing the Lancashire doorsteps until they dropped, babies fed by the side wall of the mill, bringing the money home, getting the food to the table, never giving in.[30] I carry with me the tattered remnants of this psychic structure: there is no way of not working hard, nothing but an endurance that allows you to absorb everything that comes by way of difficulty, *holding on* to the grave.

This psychology must have served capitalism at least as well as a desire for the things of the market place, which the cultural critics condemn. At least the cut-out cardboard teenage figures of Seabrook's *Working Class Childhood* know, as they sit sniffing glue and planning how to knock off a video-recorder, that the world owes them something, that they have a right to the earth, an attitude at least as potentially subversive as the passivity that arises from not ever being given very much.

Within the tradition of political and cultural criticism that this book has taken as one of its vantage points, the 1950s, the time of my own childhood, is becoming more and more frequently located as the place where the labour movement failed to place socialism on the agenda of class politics, and at the same time, failed to identify and respond to new constituencies.[31] In delineating a historical period,

the working people of that decade are seen to walk, de-
historicized, through the industrial landscape, the last of
'the old working class'. Yet within that period of time, children grew up, shaped both by the histories they inhabited
and by a modern political world.

People said at the time that the War had been fought for
the children, for a better future; and the decade represents a
watershed in the historical process by which children have
come to be thought of as repositories of hope, and objects of
desire. Accounts like Jeremy Seabrook's in *Working Class
Childhood* see in the material affection displayed towards
the children of my own and more recent generations, a
political failure on the part of the left to confront the
inculcated desires of the market place. 'Instead of the children of the working class being subjected to rigorous self-
denial for a lifetime in mill or mine,' writes Seabrook

> they have been offered instead the promise of easy and
> immediate gratification which, in the end, can sabot-
> age human development and achievement just as
> effectively as the poverty of the past.[32]

There hovers in *Working Class Childhood* the ghostly
presence of more decent and upright children, serving their
time in the restriction of poverty and family solidarity: 'the
old defensive culture of poverty gave working class children
... a sense of security which is denied the present
generation.'[33]

But in this sterner, older world the iron entered into the
children's soul, and many of them had to learn that being
alive ought simply to be enough, a gift that must ultimately
be paid for. Under conditions of material poverty, the cost
of most childhoods has been most precisely reckoned, and
only life has been given freely. It is important to note as well
that out of a childhood lived in the streets of 'the old
defensive culture of poverty', my mother brought away a
profound sense of insecurity and an incalculable longing for
the things she didn't have. She was self-indulgent and selfish

in a way that 'our mam' is not allowed to be, and she learned selfishness in the very landscape that is meant to have eradicated it in its children. She wanted things. Politics and cultural criticism can only find trivial the content of her desires, and the world certainly took no notice of them. It is one of the purposes of this book to admit her desire for the things of the earth to political reality and psychological validity.

Exclusions

The motions of desire may be legible in the text of
necessity and may then become subject to rational
explanation and criticism. But such criticism can
scarcely touch these motions at their heart . . . So
what Marxism might do, for a change, is sit on its
own head in the interest of Socialism's heart. It
might . . . cease dispensing the potions of analysis to
cure the maladies of desire. This might do good
politically as well, since it would allow a little space
not only for literary Utopias, but also for the unpre-
scribed initiatives of everyday men and women
who, in some part of themselves, are also alienated
and utopian by turn.

(E. P. Thompson, *William Morris: Romantic to
(Revolutionary)*[1]

What children learn in the course of development is that
they cannot always have what they want. The lesson can be
described as the assimilation of a set of social rules, of
prohibitions and proscriptions: it can be seen as the place
where a child enters a culture, and a culture comes to occupy
a child. But it is not clear that any child living through these
moments of denial, through the first and essential exclusion,
sees the matter in this light. What the child experiences is
loss, the loss of something that she believed she possessed, or
might possess someday, something she had a right to (these
things are as ordinary and as various as: a breast, a father, a
mother; the sense that she controls the world). The child is
excluded, cut off from something that was formerly owned

and enjoyed. Freud's re-writing of the myth of Oedipus is a highly specific account, centred on the particularity of losing a parent as a possession, of the loss that it is the fate of every human child to experience in some way or other.

If there were no history, if people were not conscious of themselves living within time and society, and if they did not use their own past to construct explanations of the present, then the myth – this particular one, others like it – could be allowed to stand, as a timeless and universal allegory of human development, and the relationship of culture to that development. But we live in time and politics, and exclusion is the promoter of envy, the social and subjective sense of the impossible unfairness of things. The first loss, the first exclusion, will be differently reinterpreted by the adult who used to be the child, according to the social circumstances she finds herself in, and the story she needs to relate.

Within Western religious and political thought, envy has long been called a sin, the improper covetousness of that to which one has no right. When Wilhelm Reich considered the formation of class-consciousness in children (and it is extremely rare to consider it as a learned position in this way) he dismissed envy as a usable motivational force, despite knowing that poverty, which naturally gave rise to envy is 'never absolute, but always relative to those who have more'.[2] Envy is thus seen as an enclosed and self-referencing system of feeling, incapable of becoming dynamic or a force from which change might spring, its only possible effect a levelling down of material and cultural life. It has usually been seen too, as the base possession of the propertyless and powerless, of the poor, and of children and women. Psychoanalysis has adopted and manipulated this general social understanding of envy, and has underlined its baseness as an impulse.

Within Kleinian analysis, envy is understood as a more primitive emotion than jealousy: out of rage at what it has lost the baby seeks to destroy that which is the very object of desire. Jealousy, on the other hand, which arises out of the oedipal triangle, is seen as much more sophisticated, propelled by love for that which is desired, and hatred for a rival. Envy though is a drive, an instinct, and will destroy what is most wanted, making reparation impossible.[3] Conceptually, in this particular account, envy in the human infant bears a strong relation to the idea of original sin.[4]

From a social viewpoint it is possible to see the most extraordinary and transparent political paternalism attaching itself to the general use of the notion within psychoanalysis. Freud was amused at the dreams of his household servant in which she replaced his wife, seeing the fantasy in the adult as a replay of the childish hopes expressed in 'Family Romances', in which children are described ridding themselves of their own parents in imagination, and replacing them with a couple altogether richer, more glamorous and powerful than their own. The replacement of the servant's dream is read through the glass of sexual attraction for the master of the house; but it did not escape the notice of either the children whom Freud observed for the writing of 'Family Romances' or of his domestic servants, that the figures of fantasy who replace the reality are actually the possessors of material goods in the material world.[5]

My mother's sense of unfairness, her belief that she had been refused entry to her rightful place in the world, was the dominant feature of her psychology and the history she told: her life itself became a demonstration of the unfairness. Thirty years after my mother passed her childhood in the North, she brought forward again and again that territory of deprivation and hardship to demonstrate the ease of our existence. The delineation of good mothering that she claimed had grown out of my grandmother's indifference was the point at which she could constantly reiterate her sense of loss, of being denied her due.

Feelings of exile and exclusion, of material and political envy, are a feature of many lives, but it is difficult to deal with them in the framework of morality outlined above. In

The Hidden Injuries of Class Richard Sennett and Jonathan Cobb make the attempt, dealing with American working life and with its subjects, adult men. Here the injuries are presented as being the result of a particular organization of the labour market and, by way of preparation for a working life, the systematic exclusions practised by school systems. Within this set of conventions, women remain hidden from view, their sense of injury related to the small-scale and the domestic.[6] The presentation of such feelings is easy, because there exists in the USA a language of material and emotional resentment outside the confining European moralities. Ordinary lives can be lived as soap opera, with each the picaresque heroine of her own hard times.[7] But here, on the other side of the Atlantic, there is no language of desire that can present what my mother wanted as anything but supremely trivial; indeed, there is no language that does not let the literal accents of class show, nor promote the tolerant yet edgy smile.

But her exile was not trivial, and she did not see it as such. The borders of her exclusion were immense; her sense of loss resolutely material: there was no point in our childhood when we were not given to understand that the experiences she described connected both with the world as it was, and the world as she wanted it to be. A recent research survey of the linguistic interaction between working-class four-year-old girls and their mothers describes the 'curriculum' of the home (it is the fate of these children in the school system that is being investigated) as wide-ranging, moving through time and space and politics, with the questions of birth and death on the agenda.[8] It is astonishing only that this finding is thought surprising. Political figures and the interstices of class were always the subject of my mother's talking to me. Churchill, she said, was a fat pig, like the rest of them, privileged and powerful; he had everything he wanted during the War: 'No rationing for him, you bet.' And then, holding the contradiction together told how 'He pulled us through. His speeches . . .'. Years later, she manicured the nails of women involved in the Profumo affair, brought home scandalous insight. Other working-class Conservative voters have been questioned over this incident and their fidelity to their party tested. Like them, she remained 'broadly permissive and indulgent', not because she thought this the right way for the upper classes to carry on, nor from reasons of deference,[9] but because she knew she was like them, or would be if only the world would let her be what she really was, and tolerance was the price she paid for knowing this. 'Still, pigs;' she said, 'they're all the same.'

She expressed the felt injuries of a social system, but analysis of her position and the position of women like her has always been seen in domestic as opposed to social terms, their political understandings imperfectly learned from men, who are full participants in the world of work.[10] Yet to deal with the felt injuries of a social system through the experience of women and girls suggests that beneath the voices of class-consciousness may perhaps lie another language, that might be heard to express the feelings of those outside the gate, the propertyless and the dispossessed. To enter the arena of subjectivity does not mean abandoning the political; indeed, to explore my mother's organization of feeling around a perception of vast personal and material inequality, political Burnley in the years between 1880 and 1920 is probably the place to start, with a description of the political culture, outlined in the last chapter, in which my mother grew and which she brought south with her, to frame and organize the social world for her own children, thirty years later.

*

In the summer of 1969, whilst working on *City Close-Up*, Jeremy Seabrook went to Blackburn and recorded his conversation with several old Lancashire weavers. They repeated over and over again, their sense of 'the unfairness of things'.[11] The phrase transfixes; and yet: there is something missing from the old weavers' tale. They remembered the tyranny of the mill, the harshness of former overseers; and it would be easy enough to believe that one heard here the expression of a shared and fully articulated experience, call it consciousness of exploitation, call it class-consciousness, and then move on. But historians of the political North-west know how unsatisfactory such labelling is, and the hold of Conservatism on the cotton towns at the turn of the century remains a problem.[12] This sense of unfairness was not necessarily translated into political understanding, nor into the politics of class, at any time over the last century. My mother's tale presents a version of this political problem: she grew to political Conservatism out of a Labour background. Her Conservatism did not express deference, nor traditionalism; nor was it the simple result of contact with rich women who could afford to have their nails painted.[13] She did not express by her political allegiance a tired acceptance of the status quo; in fact, she presented her Conservatism as radical, as a matter of defiance. The problem with this kind of defiance, whatever form it takes, is that it is rude: it disrupts conventional narratives of politics and class, and is disturbing in the way that Elizabeth Gaskell found the Lancashire mill-girls that she observed for *North and South*, who 'came rushing along, with bold fearless faces and loud laughter and jest, particularly aimed at all those who appeared to be above them in rank and station'.[14]

In the late nineteenth century, Burnley, by way of contrast with neighbouring Blackburn, still possessed a local land-owning gentry which played a prominent and traditional part in local life.[15] The most important local family were the Roman Catholic Townleys (the bluebell wood with the little stream, where I remember her last day of happiness, was Townley land), but there were others too, and their social presence in the town prevented the rise of an industrial middle class to gentry status.[16] The social rulers of Burnley were then, the traditional ones, figures of the conventional class romance; and this conservative romance and its representatives were distanced from the culture and politics of daily life: 'Burnley was known as a "Radical Hole", a Liberal dominated mill-town where land and business kept their distance.'[17]

Cotton owners remained distinct from the town's social elite, and this separation of trade from land provided a free arena for economic enterprise.[18] The establishment of a weaving business was in any case a smaller and cheaper undertaking than the setting up of a spinning shop, and since the 1850s in Burnley it had always been feasible for a cotton worker with savings to set up on his or her own. A local economic practice, which was the easy availability of rooms to rent with power for machinery thrown in, and the much-publicized facilities for saving in the town – for 'getting on' – made the possibility of rising part of its social and political landscape.[19]

Beneath the traditional form of social government represented in the separation of land and trade, a less rigid social structure pertained in Burnley when it is compared with other cotton towns. It is the argument of one historian of the town that this 'fostered greater, not less discontent, as inter-group comparisons and a wider range of reference groups became adopted'.[20] Yet within this framework, and within a social structure that allowed for individual advancement and the telling of social fairy-tales about people making good, the Burnley working class at the turn of the century seems to have shown a greater division between skilled and unskilled workers than was usual in cotton towns. This separation showed itself in the low incidence of residential contact and marriage between the two groups.[21] Burnley, then, in the early decades of this century, presented the picture of a culture in which individual aspiration and success were allowed to express themselves within the broader setting of a traditional form of local government.

The town expanded rapidly at the end of the nineteenth century, later than the other cotton towns, with the population more than doubling between 1871 and 1891.[22] Any family established during those years and maintaining a household into the new century, as did my great-grandmother, would have experienced a cycle of depression and boom. Many of my mother's uncles and aunts left the town for Fall River, Massachusetts, between the two severe depressions of 1903/4 and 1908/9, and my grandmother, age twenty-two and five-months pregnant with my mother, married my grandfather during the good year of 1913. Burnley experienced a final period of boom at the end of the First World War, before entering catastrophic recession in 1921.[23]

Through all these fluctuations in the economy, Burnley women worked: in 1911, 56 per cent of females over ten years of age were at work, most of them in the weaving sheds.[24] Work at weaving was understood as a source of pride for women, and Patrick Joyce has speculated of Burnley that 'the principal threat to the [male] weaver was perhaps that to his family authority, in work and at home . . .'[25] Yet, as has already been indicated, there were many ways in which gender divisions were maintained within the factory (particularly by the simple device of men tending a larger number of looms than women) and men received more money for work that was practically identical to that of their female fellow workers.[26]

My mother's experience of households largely supported and maintained by women was given dramatic emphasis by the death of her father at the Somme in 1916. The depression of 1921 and its aftermath changed the climate of expectation for working-class girls in the town: like many in her age group my mother did not do now, in the late 1920s, what she would have done ten years before, and go into the mill on leaving school. Her own mother stopped working in the sheds at this time because there was very little work to be had. This experience, local to Lancashire, is a specific example of a much wider social process whereby across Europe 'the importance of the mother in caring for her children . . . became much more pronounced in the early 20th century. This placed the mother at the centre of her children's affection.'[27] Children come to expect from adults what they learn to be the common practice of the adults around them. In the context of a developing domestication of women and the developing centrality of motherhood in definitions of women, a Burnley child of the 1920s felt a resentment towards a working mother who behaved less and less like the increasing number of 'new' mothers around her. Thirty years later my younger sister, who has always felt a more bitter resentment against our childhood than I do, and who has a preciser sense of what we lacked, may have learned similar new definitions of good mothering from the rapidly changing maternal practice (influenced by popularized versions of Bowlby and broadcast Winnicott) of the mid-1950s, and wanted what she did not have. Both my mother and my sister brought forward an earlier sense of psychological loss and abandonment – the first exclusion – and interpreted it, still as young children, in the light of social information and observation.

To the 'radical hole' of Burnley, immigrants arrived from rural areas much later than they did to other cotton centres. Some, from the unmechanized weaving centres of the West Riding, brought with them still-living Chartist and radical traditions, a particular perception of society organized by radicalism, and a language for expressing that perception that drew on a political understanding of the unfairness of things.[28] Political radicalism, defined as both 'a vision and analysis of social and political evils', developed in the period 1770–1850. 'It was,' observes Gareth Stedman-Jones, 'first and foremost a vocabulary of political exclusion whatever the social character of those excluded.'[29] Its rhetoric framed the demands of the Chartist movement, and as a tool of political analysis and a language of political expression, it became more and more the property of working-class people as the century advanced.[30] It is the argument of Stedman-Jones in 'Rethinking Chartism' that the development of class-consciousness later in the nineteenth century 'formed part of a language whose systematic linkages were supplied by the assumptions of radicalism: a vision and analysis of social and political evils which certainly long predated the advent of class consciousness, however defined'.[31]

Radicalism asserted the rights of the individual in conflict with privilege, privilege being seen particularly as the twin-headed hydra of Church and aristocracy. Its notable feature as a means of analysis was that its rhetoric allowed the tracing of misery, evil and unfairness to a *political* source, that is, to the manipulation by others of rights, privileges and money, rather than attributing such perception to a shared consciousness of exploitation. It was a coherent device both for understanding the ordering of the world in a particular way, and for achieving that understanding without direct *experience* of exploitation, or of a particular organization of labour, or of the vicissitudes of the labour market. This is by way of contrast with theories of class-consciousness which often do draw on such personal and direct experience, though not always explicitly.[32]

We do not, of course, know to what extent a radical vision and a radical analysis may have informed the political and social understanding of people living and working in Burnley in the period 1880–1920. But it is worth speculating, as Patrick Joyce has done for instance, about how far the perceptions of radicalism shaped the self-understanding of artisans-become-factory workers in Lancashire, cut off from former rights as individual workers over the means of production.[33] For some working people radicalism provided a means of entry to Labour politics and the politics of class;[34] it may equally have fuelled a popular Toryism.[35] Certainly, the political analysis my mother possessed and the political language she used suggest to me that her vision of the world had been organized in this way, at some point.

Burnley is a much-investigated town, and a great deal is known about political movements within it and the shaping of its political allegiances. However, two factors have been left out of the story so far. The first is any reckoning of the presence of so large a number of women in the workforce, except as adjuncts to the male story of trade unionism,[36] or in terms of a developing suffrage movement. The second missing factor is any discussion of how a political culture might affect children growing up within it. Lacking a vote, women and children have been left out of the structuring of historical analysis; but the very point of analysing a place and time in terms of a political *culture* is to assess the influence of forms of work and organization on social life and on all people's experience of that life.

The circulation of radical thought and radical rhetoric in Burnley in the late nineteenth century allows speculation about it as a set of ideas, and the meaning of these old ideas when they are brought forward into new circumstances. To say that radicalism could provide entry to socialist commitment, as it did for a very small number of working people living in Burnley, Nelson and Colne at the turn of the century, is to outline the trajectory of an accessible set of political ideas. But political ideas can be used by people in other areas of mental life, can be drawn on to help them interpret and reinterpret the world and their relationship to it. Political radicalism spoke to and for those outside the gate, the dispossessed and excluded. Such political understanding connects with subjective experiences of exile and exclusion, and political ideas like this, used to define particular circumstances (like the specific class structure of Burnley, for instance) may help bring personal ones into articulation. Possibly, in the cotton towns in the first two decades of this century, raised expectations, scepticism and resentment about what they did not possess was provoked in many women by the fact of their working in an industry which they dominated numerically, but in which they were still only women, and, in Burnley in particular, by a social structure that held out the promise of change, of advancement, of getting by and getting more, but that of course

denied its realization to the majority. The suffrage movement, which was remarkably successful in campaigning
with working women in this area, may well have been
fuelled by the substructure of envy and exclusion that the
rhetoric of radicalism provided, in the same sort of way.

Women are the shadow within modern analyses of
working-class Conservatism, and theories of deference have
been wedded to ideas about women's isolation from the
workforce, and from those formative experiences that produce class-consciousness in men, in order to explain their
position.[37] Yet my mother was not 'isolated from industrial
culture'[38] in her growing years; indeed, the argument here
has been that it was a political and industrial culture that
helped shape a sense of herself in relationship to others. The
legacy of this culture may have been her later search, in the
mid-twentieth century, for a public language that allowed
her to *want*, and to express her resentment at being on the
outside, without the material possessions enjoyed by those
inside the gate. But within the framework of conventional
political understanding, the desire for a New Look skirt
cannot be seen as a political want, let alone a proper one. We
have no better ways of understanding such manifestations
of political culture than they did in Burnley in 1908, when
they used to say dismissively that 'a motor car or carriage
would buy a woman's vote . . . at any time'.[39]

*

I have presented my own childhood, a 1950s childhood,
through the filter of my parents' story and my growing
awareness of its odd typicality, because it widens the fissure
between the terraced houses that Hoggart and Seabrook
have so lovingly described. It was a map of these streets that
my mother brought with her to use as a yardstick for our
own childhood in the post-War years. But the social world
provided other measures.

The 1950s was a time when state intervention in children's lives was highly visible, and experienced, by me at

least, as entirely beneficent. The calculated, dictated fair-
ness of the ration book went on into the new decade, and we
spent a lot of time after we moved from Hammersmith to
Streatham Hill, picking up medicine bottles of orange juice
and jars of Virol from the baby clinic for my sister. I think I
would be a very different person now if orange juice and
milk and dinners at school hadn't told me, in a covert way,
that I had a right to exist, was worth something. My
inheritance from those years is the belief (maintained always
with some difficulty) that I do have a right to the earth.[40] I
think that had I grown up with my parents only twenty years
before, I would not now believe this, for children are always
episodes in someone else's narrative, not their own people,
but rather brought into being for particular purposes. Being
a child when the state was practically engaged in making
children healthy and literate was a support against my own
circumstances, so I find it difficult to match an account of
the welfare policies of the late 1940s, which calls the
'post-War Labour government . . . the last and most glo-
rious flowering of late Victorian liberal philanthropy',
which I know to be historically correct, with the sense of self
that those policies imparted.[41] If it had been only philanthropy, would it have felt like it did? Psychic structures
are shaped by these huge historical labels: 'charity',
'philanthropy', 'state intervention'.

It was a considerable achievement for a society to pour so
much milk and so much orange juice, so many vitamins,
down the throats of its children, and for the height and
weight of those children to outstrip the measurements of
only a decade before; and this remains an achievement in
spite of the fact that the statistics of healthy and intelligent
childhood were stretched along the curve of achievement,
and only a few were allowed to travel through the narrow
gate at the age of eleven, towards the golden city. Nevertheless, within that period of time more children were provided
with the goods of the earth than had any generation been
before. What my mother lacked, I was given; and though

vast inequalities remained between me and others of my generation, the sense that a benevolent state bestowed on me, that of my own existence and the worth of that existence – attenuated, but still there – demonstrates in some degree what a fully material culture might offer in terms of physical comfort and the structures of care and affection that it symbolizes, to all its children.

What has been discussed in this chapter are matters little understood by children, but each child grows up in an adult world that is specified by both politics and social existence, and they are reared by adults who consciously know and who unconsciously manipulate the particularities of the world that shaped them. My mother's father was removed from her at the age of three by the foulest and most cynical battle of the First World War. (She remembered, she said, being lifted to the kitchen table to gaze into the face of a soldier home on leave: her father.) Forty years later, knowingly and unknowingly, she removed mine from me. It will not do to describe working-class childhood as a uniform experience, and to reserve the case-studies for the children of the upper classes. What case-studies of such childhood might reveal is a radicalized vision of society, of class-consciousness not only as a structure of feeling that arises from the relationship of people to other people within particular modes of production, but which is also an understanding of the world that can be conveyed to children; what might be called (as well as all the other names it is given) a proper envy of those who possess what one has been denied. And by allowing this envy entry into political understanding, the proper struggles of people in a state of dispossession to gain their inheritance might be seen not as sordid and mindless greed for the things of the market place, but attempts to alter a world that has produced in them states of unfulfilled desire.

But to use such evidence, the evidence of all the unwritten case-histories, involves a difficult double vision. What has been made in this way is a product of material and psychological deprivation: the subjects of these histories are made what they are out of multiple poverties, and what they do in the course of development is an aspect of their social and cultural marginality: these are sad and secret stories.

Histories

> Pointless stories are met with the withering rejoin-
> der, 'So what?' Every good narrator is continually
> warding off this question; when his narrative is over
> it should be unthinkable for a bystander to say 'So
> what?'
>
> (William Labov, *Language in the Inner City*)[1]

I grew up in a culture and at a time when it was easy to place
childhood on a developmental map. My mother, using both
the transmitted child psychology of the 1950s and much
older notions of what children could do or could be expected to do when they reached a certain age, knew when I
stopped being a child. Understanding human development
in this particular way is a fairly recent cultural achievement,
and it is still somewhat shaky in its application after baby-
hood is passed, especially where female children are concerned, with little girls often seen to embody the physical
virtues of the ideal woman: narcissism, containment, clarity
of flesh, large eyes and slenderness. Little boys, by way of
contrast, are frequently understood to possess an adult
masculinity as soon as they emerge from infancy. Steven
Marcus in 'Freud and Dora: Story, History, Case-History'
has pointed out that the late nineteenth century Viennese
physician had a great deal of trouble in siting his eighteen-
year-old hysterical patient in the tables of physiological and
sexual growth:

> he is . . . utterly uncertain about where Dora is, or was
> developmentally. At one moment in the passage he

> calls her a 'girl', at another a 'child' – but in point of
> fact he treats her throughout as if this fourteen- six-
> teen- and eighteen-year-old adolescent had the capaci-
> ties for sexual response of a grown woman.[2]

Examples of this uncertainty abound in all sociological
and literary accounts of nineteenth-century girlhood.[3]
William Thackeray, for example, addressed thus the
sixteen-year-old daughter of an American acquaintance
in the 1850s:

> If I were to come there now, I wonder should I be
> allowed to come and see you in your nightcap – I
> wonder even if you wear a nightcap? I should step up,
> take your little hand, which I daresay is lying outside
> the coverlet, give it a little shake, and then sit down
> and talk all sorts of stuff and nonsense to you for half
> an hour.[4]

This uncertainty about development and sexuality also
extended to very young girls – to children – and to those of
the working class. Henry Mayhew, collecting material for a
series of articles in the *Morning Chronicle* in 1849/50, and
transcribing the conversations that were later to make up
London Labour and the London Poor, interviewed an
eight-year-old street-trader in watercresses and frankly recorded his confusion about her place on the developmental
map: 'the little watercress girl . . . although only eight years
of age had already lost all childish ways, was indeed, in
thoughts and manner, a woman . . .'.[5] The little girl herself
knew that she occupied some place between childhood and
adulthood, and told the social investigator that 'I ain't a
child, and I shan't be a woman till I'm twenty, but I'm past
eight, I am.' Mayhew mused on her status: 'I did not know
how to talk with her,' he recorded; and Freud, after Dora's
last visit, did 'not know what kind of help she wanted from
me';[6] both of them transfixed by the determinations of
femininity, both seduced in spite of themselves, the one
moved by compassion, the other by the manipulations of
hysteria.

Dora and the little watercress girl are of use here because they both told stories, that is, each of them had an auto-biography to impart, and they did so through the agency of the interest and inquiry of two investigators of the human condition. They are divided by age, by class, by time and geography, and the content of their stories seems different too, in so far as each represents a different social reality. They are held together, however, not only by the dichot-omous nature of their two narratives and the way in which one illuminates the other, but by being young girls, occupy-ing the contradictory and categorically diffuse place between infancy and womanhood. Dora's and the little watercress girl's stories are used here because they are rare autobiographical accounts of femininity: the little watercress girl, in fact, presents an almost unique piece of evidence about working-class childhood. The two accounts taken together bring into focus certain themes of this book; and in the making of history what evidence presents itself must be used, in spite of the chronological disturbance it suggests (London in the 1850s, Vienna in the 1900s); the making of history might, in fact, be seen as the theorization of such disruption and dislocation. This final chapter, then, is concerned with the relationship between the autobiographical account (the personal history), case-history, and the construction and writing of history. It is about women's history, as indeed this book is, about the difficulties of writing it, the other stories that get in the way, and different kinds of narrative form.

Within this enterprise, childhood is at once revelatory and problematic. Working-class childhood is problematic be-cause of the many ways in which it has been pathologized over the last century and a half.[7] In the romantic construc-tion of childhood, which propelled the earliest child-study and within which the psychoanalytic enterprise must place itself, the children of the poor are only a measure of what they lack as children: they are a falling-short of a more complicated and richly endowed 'real' child; though that real child may suffer all the vicissitudes of neurosis. Child analysis was a late manifestation of the romantic quest to establish childhood as an area of experience lying within us all, not as a terrain abandoned, but as a landscape of feeling that might be continually reworked and reinterpreted.[8] The appropriation of these ideas – both romantic and literary, and technical – to general social understanding, has tended to de-historicize childhood, has allowed it to be seen as existing in and of itself. Yet childhood *is* a kind of history, the continually reworked and re-used personal history that lies at the heart of each present. What is brought forward for interpretation is structured by its own figurative devices, arranged according to the earliest perceptions of the entities in the real world that give us our metaphors, and the social reality and meaning that metaphor co-joins.

*

Henry Mayhew encountered the eight-year-old watercress-seller in the East End of London, probably in the Farringdon area, sometime in the winter of 1849/50. Of all the little girls he interviewed during this winter and over the next ten years, she was the one who touched him the most: he was puzzled by her, he pitied her, he felt affection for her; she was not like the children he knew, and yet she was a child. He was attracted by her, and repelled at the same time:

> There was something cruelly pathetic in hearing this infant, so young that her features had scarcely formed themselves, talking of the bitterest struggles of life, with the calm earnestness of one who has endured them all. At first I treated her as a child, speaking on childish subjects; so that I might, by being familiar with her, remove all shyness and get her to relate her life freely . . .

The method did not work; the child would not be treated as a child; 'a look of amazement soon put an end to any attempt at fun' on Mayhew's part. However, the child did have a story to tell, and she eventually related it, moving back in time from her current position, after some preliminary remarks:

> I go about the street with watercresses, crying 'Four bunches a penny, watercresses.' I am just eight years old – that's all, and I've a big sister, and a brother, and a sister younger than I am. On and off I've been very near a twelvemonth on the streets. Before that I used to take care of a baby for my aunt. I . . . minded it for ever such a long time – till it could walk . . . Before I had the baby, I used to help mother, who was in the fur trade; and if there was any slits in the fur I'd sew them up. My mother learned me to needlework and knit when I was about five. I used to go to school too; but I wasn't there long. I've forgotten all about it now, it's such a long time ago . . .

From this sequentially accurate (though chronologically reversed) account, the child selected certain themes – her relationship with her parents and siblings, the financial organization of her life, the questions of play and enjoyment that she had formerly denied – and elaborated on them for the benefit of her interlocutor.[9] These themes, which were central to the child's understanding of herself, will be returned to later.

Some fifty years later, in another European city, Freud encountered the upper-middle-class hysteric 'Dora' (in reality, Ida Bauer) who was brought to him by her father at various points during her adolescence in the hope of curing her of coughing attacks, loss of voice, depression and various other nervous symptoms. The implicit expectation was also that the analyst would be able to cure her of a view of her social and sexual reality that did not suit her father, who was at this time and who had for several years past been adulterously involved with the wife of a family friend, called 'Frau K.' in the case-history.[10]

At several points during the four years before she started analysis with Freud, Dora had come to believe that there was a tacit agreement between her father and the husband of her father's mistress, to hand her over to Herr. K. as the trade-off for the adulterous relationship. 'When she was feeling embittered,' recorded Freud

> she used to be overcome by the idea that she had been handed over to Herr K. as the price of his tolerating the relations between her father and his wife; and her rage at her father's making such a use of her was visible behind her affection for him. At other times she was quite aware that she had been guilty of exaggeration in talking like this. The two men had never of course made a formal agreement in which she was an object for barter.[11]

There are several accounts of the case-study available, and indeed, 'Fragment of an Analysis of a Case of Hysteria' is one of the most widely read of Freud's works.[12] The account above, then, is the merest outline of the case itself, and what follows is not concerned with Dora's hysteria, nor with Freud's failure to cure it, nor with her relentless desire to present to her analyst the validity of her own version of events. It is rather concerned with the questions raised by the presentation of personal stories, the relationship of those narratives to history, and above all with the question that Ida Bauer herself raised so explicitly eighty years ago, that of the exchange of women in modern Western society. If we are able to move the idea of the traffic in women through time, space and culture, move it from remote and pre-capitalist societies to our own, and see it as a valid label for subjective experience, then this is largely to do with the evidence that Dora so clearly laid on the table, and that Freud interpreted for us.

Using these two accounts, we may suddenly see the nineteenth century peopled by middle-aged men who, propelled by the compulsions of scientific inquiry, demanded stories from young women and girls; and then expressed their dissatisfaction with the form of the narratives they obtained. Freud began his treatment of Dora by asking her 'to give me the whole story of [her] life and illness'.[13] It was the unsatisfactory nature of this first narrative that usually allowed the analyst to 'see [his] way about the case': it was with the gaps, the inconclusive narrative connections, the hesitations and spontaneous revisions as to date, time and place, that the patient presented clues to where the true account lay:

> The patient comes with the story of his or her own life. The analyst listens; through an association something intrudes, disrupts, offers the 'anarchic carnival' back into that history, the story won't quite do, and so the process starts again. You go back, and you make a new history.[14]

It has been suggested that in his writing of this particular case-study Freud implied that 'everyone – that every life, every existence – has a story;' and that the story the hysteric tells presents dramatic shortcomings as narrative. 'What we are forced at this juncture to conclude,' remarks Steven Marcus

> is that a coherent story is in some manner connected with mental health . . . and that this in turn provides assumptions of the broadest and deepest kind about both the nature of coherence and the form and structure of human life. On this reading, human life is, ideally, a connected and coherent story, with all the details in explanatory order and with everything . . . accounted for, in its proper causal or other sequence.[15]

What a successful analyst might do is to give the analysand possession of her own story, and that possession would be 'a final act of appropriation, the appropriation by oneself of ones own history'.[16]

Some of Freud's earliest efforts in his short treatment of Dora were directed towards demonstrating that she did not say what she meant, that she was in fact attracted by Herr K., but was unwilling to acknowledge her own desire. He concentrated particularly on an event that took place when the girl was sixteen and, out alone on a holiday walk with the man, was propositioned by him. She slapped his face, hurried away, and on telling her parents about the incident, was met with disbelief – or a kind of feigned and socially appropriate disbelief.[17] Freud recognized that what obsessed Dora was her father's apparent willingness to believe that this scene by the lake was just 'a figment of her imagination. She was almost beside herself at the idea of its being supposed that she had merely fancied something on that occasion.'[18]

Later, in his revision of the case-study for publication, Freud concluded that 'Dora's story must correspond to the facts in every respect;'[19] but it is not clear that he acknowledged its validity at the time. What Dora needed to do was to demonstrate to him that she had been right, and two years after her analysis terminated she returned to Freud's consulting room on the pretext of asking for further help, but in fact to tell him that she had extracted confessions of adultery from Frau K. and 'an admission of the scene by the lake that [Herr K.] had disputed'.[20]

The failure in narrative that it has been suggested Freud attributed to Dora was not in fact a failure of which he always accused his patients. Indeed, in a later case-study, that of the Wolf Man, there is a clear implication that narrative truth, order and sequence does not much signify in the eliciting of a life history, for it must remain the same story in the end, that is, the individual's account of how she got to be the way she is.[21] To concentrate on narrative sequence is to ignore the transactional nature of individual narratives. Narratives are a means of exchange. People may remember the past, and may verbalize their recollections, but to become a story what they say must 'achieve a coherence and point which are the same for the hearer as the teller'.[22] Dora's early accounts did not become stories because the point of the situation in which they were delivered was to present her with an account that was different from her own, to give her, in fact, Freud's story of Dora.

After the scene at the lake, two years before her analysis

with Freud started, Dora had had a recurring dream which she later recounted to him:

> A house was on fire. My father was standing beside my bed and woke me up. I dressed myself quickly. Mother wanted to stop and save her jewel-case; but father said: "I refuse to let myself and my children be burnt for the sake of your jewel-case.' We hurried down-stairs, and soon as I was outside, I woke up.[23]

This dream of the 1890s has been taken through many interpretations that move far beyond the one that Freud originally made. An essential feature of all of them though, is the attention that Freud paid at the time to the connection between the German word for jewel-case (*Schmuck-kastchen*) and its slang meaning, which is a name for the female genitals.[24] Some time before the 'scene' and the dream, Herr K. had given Dora an expensive jewel-case. 'Bring your mind back to the jewel-case,' suggested Freud.

> You have there a starting point for a ... line of thoughts in which Herr K. is to be put in the place of your father just as he was in the matter of standing beside your bed. He gave you a jewel-case; so now you are to give him your jewel-case ... you are ready to give to Herr K. what his wife withholds from him.[25]

The role of the mother in the dream is problematic in Freud's analysis of it, as Maria Ramas has pointed out. In 'Freud's Dora, Dora's Hysteria', she suggests that Frau Bauer, Ida's mother, saw heterosexuality as representative of contamination, in particular of venereal infection, and that her desire to save her jewel-case in her daughter's dream about the fire, was a repudiation of sexual intercourse and any man's gift – an understanding that Dora had appropri-ated and which she presented to Freud as her own.[26]

When he came to write his final version of the case-study, Freud was willing to admit social meaning and sociological reality to the narrative:

> It follows from the nature of the facts which form the
> material of psycho-analysis that we are obliged to pay
> as much attention in our case-histories to the purely
> human and social circumstances of our patients as to
> the somatic data and the symptoms of the disorder.[27]

He has been condemned for this in analytic terms [28] but it is
entirely due to his recording of social detail and social
interpretation that Ida Bauer's evidence can be used as
historical evidence. Dora understood two things about her
social and sexual worth. She knew that she was desired and
that she might be thought of as an object of exchange
between two men. She knew also, with great specificity,
what it was that was the subject of exchange: not herself,
but her genitals, not a person, but what that person possessed, which was her sex: an object, a valuable item, a thing
to be bought and sold. The metaphor that Freud used for
interpretation draws on no perceptible connection between
genitals and jewel-cases, but rather on a highly specific and
powerfully represented *connection* between middle- and
upper-class women and their value on the market and in the
social world. That, in time and place, was Dora's value,
what she understood of herself because the world told her so
(Freud too, as part of that world, told her this); and it was
this knowledge that she tried to repudiate by her hysteria.[29]

*

The little watercress girl on the other hand, possessed
nothing, except her labour, and her story, which was coherent, and ordered, though told in reverse sequence. Her
interlocutor did not accuse her of narrative inconsistencies
and lacunae, of denials and repressions (Mayhew was not
listening for them); what Mayhew found fault with was not
her story (for unlike Freud, who already knew Dora's story,
Mayhew did not know the tale this child told) but herself,
and the blank absence of childhood from her face. The child
knew that there was a point to the tale she told (and
Mayhew allowed her her point of view) and performed the

device known among narratologists as 'the *evaluation* of the narrative: the means used by the narrator to indicate the point of the narrative, its *raison d'être*, why it was told and what the narrator was getting at'.[30] Within these strictly sociolinguistic terms, evaluation is to do with dramatization, that is, the eventual presentation of a dramatic *point* to the story, such as a fight. But the little watercress girl made the same gesture of evaluation in order to reach a different kind of conclusion: the point of her story was herself, and how that self had been made.

What the child chose to extract from her autobiographical narrative and to comment on was the financial ordering of her household, and the way in which her labour was managed and controlled by her mother. The personal relationships she described were all bound by this economic vision. She talked in some detail about a Saturday job that she did for a Jewish couple, and about her career as a baby-minder. She had in her short lifetime looked after a nephew or a niece, and was still engaged in looking after her baby sister. Child care represented paid employment, and even in looking after her sister she was performing a function that would have had cash laid out on it by her mother had she not existed.[31] The child understood herself to be in this way a worker, and described her working life with great exactitude:

> Sometimes I make a great deal of money. One day I took 1s 6d and the cresses cost 6d,[32] but it isn't often that I make as much as that. I oftener make 3d or 4d than 1s; and then I'm at work crying 'Cresses, four bunches a penny, cresses!' from six in the morning till about ten . . . The shops buys most of me. Some of 'em says 'Oh, I ain't a goin to give a penny for these;' and they want them at the same price I buys 'em at. I always gives mother my money, she's so very good to me . . . She's very poor and goes out cleaning rooms sometimes, now she doesn't work at the fur.[33] I ain't got no father, he's a father in law. No, mother ain't married again – he's a father in law. He grinds scissors

and he's very good to me. No; I don't mean by that
that he says kind things to me for he never hardly
speaks . . . I am a capital hand at bargaining . . . they
can't take me in. If the woman tries to give me a small
handful of cresses I says 'I ain't a goin to have that for a
ha'porth,' and I goes to the next basket, and so on, all
round. I know the quantities very well. For a penny I
ought to have a full market hand . . . For 3d I has a lap
full, enough to earn about a shilling; and for 6d I gets
as many as crams my basket . . . When I've bought 3d
of cresses, I ties 'em up into as many little bundles as I
can. They must look biggish, or the people won't buy
them.

It is clear that under the conditions of distress that her family
experienced, she received the most praise and approbation
from the adults around her when she made 4d profit out of a
bundle of watercress. Her labour functioned as a description of herself – or rather, she used it as a description of what
she knew herself to be – and the babies she minded show this
metaphoric use she made of her own labour most clearly. In
the little watercress girl's account, the baby was both a
source of love and affection, a means of play and enjoyment
(she spoke of the warmth of a small body in bed at night, the
pleasurable weight of her baby sister on her hip, the smiles
of infancy); and at the same time the baby was also a source
of income and adult praise for earning that income. The
baby represented economically what the watercress seller
had been in her turn, when she was a baby, and what she
was now to her mother: a worker, a good and helpful little
girl, a source of income. In this situation her labour was not
an attribute, nor a possession, but herself; that which she
exchanged daily for the means of livelihood, for love, and
food and protection. It was in the face of this integrity of
being that Mayhew felt undone.

*

The child did possess something after all, she told the
social investigator, quite late during the course of their

conversation: some toys: 'Oh yes; I've got some toys at home. I've a fireplace and a box of toys, and a knife and fork and two little chairs . . .' Perhaps presented by Mayhew for the purposes of demonstrating pathos (did she really have play-furniture, or was she, out of her confusion and deprivation, describing her family's limited stock of household goods?), toys, the possible symbols of easier childhoods, rest uneasily in a reading of the child's account. Toys belong to a world of things that we know immensely and conventionally about; the watercresses though, the pieces of fur with the slits to sew up, the pennies saved for clothes, are not only strange entities, but the connections made between them remain unrevealed by our reading.

It is generally recognized in literary accounts of metaphor, that the connective device on which metaphor turns, that is, on the perception of real similarities between entities in the real world, is often in actuality no more than the recognition of culturally highly specific contingent relations: we are used to comparing certain things with particular other things, and metaphor often works through this connection, rather than perceived similarity. Reading literature from unfamiliar cultures often serves to reveal the conventions of our own metaphoric system, for we do not have forty-three names for the eagle, nor a gradation of terms to describe the colour of snow. 'There is scant physical basis for comparing women with swans,' remarks Jonathan Culler on this point; but we are massively used to reading the comparison as metaphor.[34]

In Dora's account the contingencies of our understanding furnish almost everything (it is a world we know about, a real world, a big house, by a lake, or behind a gate: this story has been told before; it is *the* story). There are things (entities, relationships, people: names) and there is the placing of things in relationship to each other, which give them their meaning. When a thing is presented in Dora's story, it takes on a universe of meaning: a jewel-case, a reticule, a closed door, a pair of pearl ear-rings. In this way, the writing of case-history takes on the dimensions of story-telling: it works by telling us that something is about to be revealed – that the story is already there to tell.

But there is no story for the little watercress girl. The things she spoke to Mayhew about (pieces of fur, the bunches of cress, the scrubbed floor) still startle after 130 years, not because they are strange things in themselves, but because in our conventional reading, they are not held together in figurative relationship to each other. According to some authorities, both narrative and metaphor work by bringing together things that at first seem separate and distant, but which then, moved towards each other through logical space, make a new and pertinent sense. But this shift through space depends on our ability as listeners and readers to accept the new ordering of events and entities which have been made by the plot of a story, or by the use of a metaphor. Where there is not the vision that permits the understanding of these new connections, then a story cannot be told.

Those who have pointed to the social specificity of the personal accounts around which psychoanalysis constructed itself have also been talking about the conventions of story-telling and story-reading that have confined it. Jane Gallop has discussed the position of the maid, the nurse and the governess in classic psychoanalysis, the figure who relates the idealized and isolated family of the late nineteenth-century case-histories to the economic world, but who has always been denied a place in them.[35] In *In Search of a Past*, an autobiography structured by psychoanalytic inquiry, Ronald Fraser replaces the servants in the manor house of his own childhood – in all the haunted houses – gives them a voice, fills the place that classic psychoanalysis cannot discuss.[36] But even with this replacement, the narrative continues to work in the same way, telling a story that we know already.

In the narrative terms that Freud can be seen to have laid down in 'Fragment of an Analysis', the little watercress girl is a person in mental health, in possession of her story. But it is the story itself that does not fit: all its content and its imagery demonstrate its marginality to the central story, of the bourgeois household and the romances of the family and the fairy-tales that lie behind its closed doors: no different culture here, not a place where they have forty-three terms for the eagle and where a woman cannot be conceived of as a swan; but the arena outside the gate, the set of metaphors forged out of the necessary and contingent relationship between all the big houses and the Clerkenwell rooms in which the child grew up. The marginality of her story is what maintains the other's centrality; there is no kind of narrative that can hold the two together (though perhaps history can): an outsider's tale, held in oscillation by the relationships of class.

*

She was free, and she was not free. Her father didn't matter, he didn't represent any law: he was just a 'father in law'. The law, the distant functioning world, was the gentleman who stopped her once in the street, not to pity her, but to ask why she was out so early, and who gave her nothing. It was the inexorable nature of the market, the old women whole-salers, some kind, some not. She was free; she was hungry, meat made her feel sick, she was so unused to it. She had integrity; and she was very poor. Her matted and dirty hair stood out wildly from her head, she shuffled along to keep the carpet slippers on her feet; her life slipped away into the darkness, as she turned into the entrance of her Clerkenwell court.

Childhood for a Good Woman

That time, the last time, when she opened the door, she looked like a witch. I've tried to explain this often to friends, to say what this sudden perception means. There was a new children's paperback out, a version of 'Hansel and Gretal' in modern dress, that I'd recently seen.[1] A witch opens the door of the gingerbread house; she stands there; you look at her face: she is like my mother. I've explained often that our imagining of witches is based on a certain real and physiological type of woman, on a Lancashire face, with dark hair and dark eyes, and handsome, gaunt curves to the cheek and nose. That was how my mother looked, and the illness made her thinner and gaunter. Witchcraft endured in Lancashire much later than in other parts of the country; community tensions between Catholic and Protestant, ownership and exclusion, fuelled it as a popular political device.[2]

She talked to me about witches, now and often before. The one book she carried from her childhood was Ainsworth's *Lancashire Witches*, in an edition of the 1880s.[3] She'd walked by Pendle Hill she said, to dances in the 1920s, by the place where Mistress Nutter met her fellow witches, and where the witches were later burned. I found the book in the house after her death, remembered my terrified reading of it at the age of ten, convinced that the mere opening of its pages brought the devil forward.

She wanted to tell me about Lancashire witchcraft I think, because it put her pursuit of the invulnerable body through Food Reform into a kind of historical perspective, gave it a tradition. She did not make the connection clear, but did talk about the doctor who had attended her when she'd had diphtheria at the age of ten, who'd recommended dried fruit and wholemeal bread, food with properties she'd discovered herself, later in life.

Talk of witchcraft was common in north-east Lancashire in the 1890s, and the connection of Food Reform and herbalism with radical politics in the area is a matter of historical knowledge.[4] What she did, it is clear, is understand her search for spells, for the food that nourished – a kind of magic – in a historical light. Time catches together what we know and what we do not yet know. She thought she might save her life by eating watercress, the food of clear water grown in the distant hills, far away from a useless present. The little watercress girl knew nothing of where the cresses came from. My mother did what the powerless, particularly powerless women, have done before, and do still: she worked on her body, the only bargaining power she ended up with, given the economic times and the culture in which she grew.

She made me believe that I understood everything about her, she made me believe that I was her: her tiredness, the pain of having me, the bleeding, the terrible headaches. She made me good because I was a spell, a piece of possible good fortune, a part of herself that she exchanged for her future: a gamble. If you expect children to be self-sacrificing and to identify with the needs of others, then they often do so, and cannot restrict their identification to one other person. They may even find themselves much later, unknowingly, in their mirror image, in the little watercress girl, the good and helpful child, who eased her mother's life. Whenever I cry over that child, I think what a fool she would think me to waste my tears in this way. She doesn't know that there are means of escape. You can open the books, and see the witch's face that others have seen before, find a story that shows the witch making the rose trees sink into the ground, or the witch flying over Pendle Hill. And then you can turn the page: read on.

It was two weeks before her death that I went to see her that time, the last time: the first meeting in nine years, except for the day of my father's funeral. The letter announcing my visit lay unopened on the mat when she opened the door; and an hour later I came away believing that I admired a woman who could, in these circumstances and in some pain, treat me as if I had just stepped round the corner for a packet of tea ten minutes before, and talk to me about this and that, and nothing at all. But I was really a ghost who came to call. That feeling, the sense of being absent in my mother's presence, was nothing to do with the illness, was what it had always been like. We were truly illegitimate, outside any law of recognition: the mirror broken, a lump of ice for a heart.

As I went out, past the shrouded furniture in the front room (things made ready these ten years past for the move that never came), I saw hanging over the mantelpiece a Lowry reproduction that hadn't been there on my last visit. Why did she go out and buy that obvious representation of a landscape she wanted to escape, the figures moving noiselessly under the shadow of the mill? 'They know each other, recognise each other,' says John Berger of these figures. 'They are not, as is sometimes said, like lost souls in limbo; they are fellow travellers through a life which is impervious to most of their choices . . .' Perhaps, as this commentary suggests, she did buy that picture because it is 'concerned with loneliness', with the 'contemplation of time passing without meaning',[5] and moved then, hesitantly, momentarily, towards all the other lost travellers.

*

Where is the place that you move into the landscape and can see yourself? When I want to find myself in the dream of the New Look, I have to reconstruct the picture, look down at my sandals and the hem of my dress, for in the dream itself, I am only an eye watching. Remembering the visit to the cotton mill, on the other hand, I can see myself watching from the polished floor: I am in the picture. To see yourself in this way is a representation of the child's move into historical time, one of the places where vision establishes the child's understanding of herself as part of the world. In its turn, this social understanding helps interpret the dream landscape.

When I was about nine, I grew positively hungry for poetry. I learned enormous quantities to say to myself in bed at night. The book I had was Stevenson's *A Child's Garden of Verses*, and I read it obsessively, once going into Smith's in the High Road to ask if he'd written any other poems. I liked the one on the last page best, 'To Any Reader', and its imparting of the sad, elegiac information that the child seen through the pages of the book

> . . . has grown up and gone away,
> And it is but a child of air
> That lingers in the garden there.

You're nostalgic for childhood whilst it's happening to you, because the dreams show you the landscape you're passing through, but you don't know yet that you want to escape.

*

Once a story is told, it ceases to be a story: it becomes a piece of history, an interpretative device. Long, long ago, the fairy-stories were my first devices. Thirty years after my intensest reading of Hans Andersen, I learned that he was an outcast, a poor man intent on pleasing his patrons and recording messages of embourgeoisement.[6] It is significant that Andersen, a working-class writer edgy in the upper-middle-class and gentry world of nineteenth-century Denmark should have presented so many dramas concerning women: the dazzling and powerful Snow Queen, Gerda who looks relentlessly for the cypher Kay along the edges of the world, the Little Mermaid, a thousand witches of the sea. Women are the final outsiders, and Andersen wrote his own drama of class using their names, thus demonstrating a rare reversal of a common transformation of gender in reading, whereby girls have to read themselves as boys in order to become active heroines in the text.

Using devices like this, the story forms. I know that the compulsions of narrative are almost irresistible: having found a psychology where once there was only the assumption of pathology or false consciousness to be seen, the tendency is to celebrate this psychology, to seek entry for it to a wider world of literary and cultural reference; and the enterprise of working-class autobiography was designed to make this at least a feasible project. But to do this is to miss the irreducible nature of all our lost childhoods: what has been made has been made out on the borderlands. I must make the final gesture of defiance, and refuse to let this be absorbed by the central story; must ask for a structure of political thought that will take all of this, all these secret and impossible stories, recognize what has been made out on the margins; and then, recognizing it, refuse to celebrate it; a politics that will, watching this past say 'So what?'; and consign it to the dark.

Notes

The place of publication is London, unless otherwise specified. The abbreviation PP stands for the Parliamentary Paper Series.

Death of a Good Woman

1. Simone de Beauvoir, *A Very Easy Death* (1964), Penguin, 1969, p. 83.

PART ONE: STORIES

1. John Berger, *About Looking*, Writers and Readers, 1972, pp. 370–1.
2. Gareth Stedman-Jones, 'Why is the Labour Party in a Mess?' in *Languages of Class: Studies in English Working Class History, 1832–1982*, Cambridge University Press, Cambridge, 1983, pp. 239–56. Beatrix Campbell surveys critiques of the 1950s in *Wigan Pier Revisited*, Virago, 1984, pp. 217–34. See also James Hinton, *Labour and Socialism: A History of the British Labour Movement, 1867–1974*, Wheatsheaf, Brighton, 1983, pp. 182–7.
3. 'What actually happened is less important than what is felt to have happened. Is that right?' says Ronald Fraser to his analyst, and his analyst agrees. Ronald Fraser, *In Search of a Past*, Verso, 1984, p. 95.
4. Jeremy Seabrook, *Working Class Childhood*, Gollancz, 1982, pp. 23–7, 33.
5. Catherine Cookson, *Our Kate*, Macdonald, 1969.
6. Kathleen Woodward, *Jipping Street* (1928), Virago, 1983.

7. Seabrook, op. cit., p. 140.

8. Richard Hoggart, *The Uses of Literacy*, Penguin, 1959, p. 91.

9. Jeremy Seabrook, *The Unprivileged* (1967), Penguin, 1973, Foreword.

10. ibid., pp. 202–3.

11. Sally Alexander, 'Women, Class and Sexual Difference', *History Workshop Journal*, 17 (1984), pp. 125–49. Karl Marx, 'Preface to "A Contribution to the Critique of Political Economy"' (1859), *Early Writings*, The Pelican Marx Library, Penguin, 1975, pp. 424–8.

12. George Lukas, *History and Class Consciousness*, Merlin Press, 1968, pp. 46–82, especially pp. 50–5. See also Eric Hobsbawm, 'Notes on Class Consciousness', in *Worlds of Labour*, Weidenfeld and Nicolson, 1984, pp. 15–32.

13. Lukas, op. cit., p. 51.

14. Pauline Hunt, *Gender and Class Consciousness*, Macmillan, 1980, pp. 171–9. A direct and simple learning isn't posited here; but it is the workplace and an existing backdrop of trade-union organization that provides for the expression of women's class consciousness.

15. Alexander, op. cit., p. 131.

16. See below, 'Exclusions', pp. 119–21; and Gareth Stedman-Jones, 'Rethinking Chartism' in Stedman-Jones, op. cit., pp. 90–178.

17. Hoggart, op. cit., p. 293.

18. Jeremy Seabrook, *What Went Wrong?*, Gollancz, 1978, pp. 260–61.

19. ibid., p. 262.

20. To be told how difficult it was to give birth to you is an extremely common experience for all little girls, and as John and Elizabeth Newson point out in *Seven Years Old in the Home Environment*, Allen & Unwin, 1976, pp. 186–7, chaperonage, and the consequent amount of time girls spend in adult company, is likely to make such topics of conversation accessible to them. But the punishment and the warning involved in telling girl children about the difficulties their birth presented to their mother is rarely written about. But see Carolyn Steedman, *The Tidy House: Little Girls Writing*, Virago, 1982, pp. 34–5, 145–7.

21. Ursula Owen (ed.), *Fathers: Reflections by Daughters*, Virago, 1983. Ann Oakley, *Taking It Like a Woman*, Cape, 1984.

22. E. Ann Kaplan, 'Is the Gaze Male?', in Ann Snitow *et al.* (eds), *Desire: The Politics of Female Sexuality*, Virago, 1984, p. 335.

23. Jane Gallop, *Feminism and Psychoanalysis: The Daughter's Seduction*, Macmillan, 1982, p. xv.

24. For recent arguments concerning the necessity of historicization, see Jane Lewis, 'The Debate on Sex and Class', *New Left Review*, 149 (1985), pp. 108–20.

25. Michael Young and Peter Willmott, *Family and Kinship in East London*, Penguin, 1962, pp. 44–61.

26. Raymond Williams, *Politics and Letters*, NLB/Verso, 1979, pp. 271–2. See also Seabrook, *What Went Wrong?*, p. 261, where the same process is described: a working-class life, ossified by time, enacted in 'symbolic institutional ways, by those who teach in poor schools, or who write novels and memoirs about a way of life which they have not directly experienced since childhood'.

27. Seymour Chatman, *Story and Discourse: Narrative Structure in Fiction and Film*, Cornell University Press, 1978, pp. 45–8.

28. See Steven Marcus, 'Freud and Dora: Story, History, Case-History', in *Representations*, Random House, New York, 1976, pp. 247–310 for the argument that Freud invented a new narrative form in his writing of the 'Dora' case. See also below, pp. 130–4.

29. For a brief discussion of the way in which historical writing masks the processes that brought it into being, see Timothy Ashplant, 'The New Social Function of Cinema', *Journal of the British Film Institute*, 79/80 (1981), pp. 107–9, and Hayden White, 'The Value of Narrativity in the Representation of Reality', *Critical Inquiry*, 7:1 (1980), pp. 5–27.

30. Paul Ricoeur, *Time and Narrative*, University of Chicago Press, Chicago, 1984, pp. 118, 157.

31. Ann Oakley, *From Here to Maternity: Becoming a Mother*, Penguin, 1981, p. 11.

32. Campbell, op. cit., pp. 97–115.

33. John Berger, *Ways of Seeing*, BBC/Penguin, 1972, p. 46.

34. Donald Winnicott, *Playing and Reality*, Penguin, 1974, p. 6.

PART TWO: EXILES

The Weaver's Daughter

1. George Herriman's Krazy Kat cartoons, syndicated throughout the USA from '1913 onwards, are reproduced in *Krazy Kat Komix*, vols 1–4, Real Free Press, Amsterdam, 1974–5.
2. That is, never applied to the parish authorities for financial assistance under the Poor Law.
3. Jill Liddington and Jill Norris, *One Hand Tied Behind Us: The Rise of the Women's Suffrage Movement*, Virago, 1978.
4. Samuel Bamford, *Early Days*, 1849, quoted in David Vincent, *Bread, Knowledge and Freedom*, Methuen, 1981, p. 92.
5. Richard Hoggart mentions the sum of £8 a week as an extravagant amount to spend on housekeeping in 1956/7. *Uses of Literacy*, p. 43.
6. Frederic Jameson, *The Political Unconscious*, Methuen, 1981, pp. 155–7. V. S. Naipaul, *A House for Mr Biswas*, André Deutsch, 1961. See *New York Review of Books*, 24 November 1983, for Naipaul's description of writing the book in Streatham Hill.

PART THREE: INTERPRETATIONS

Living Outside the Law

1. Juliet Mitchell, *Psychoanalysis and Feminism*, Penguin, 1975, pp. 394–5.
2. Quoted in Carolyn Steedman, *The Tidy House: Little Girls Writing*, Virago, 1982, p. 99.
3. Lily Pincus and Christopher Dare, *Secrets in the Family*, Faber & Faber, 1978, pp. 9–10.
4. See 'Histories', pp. 129–34.
5. Gayle Rubin, 'The Traffic in Women: Notes on the "Political Economy" of Sex', in Rayna R. Reiter (ed.), *Towards an Anthropology of Women*, Monthly Reviews Press, New York, 1975, pp. 157–210.
6. ibid., p. 189. E. P. Thompson, *The Making of the English Working Class*, Penguin, 1968, pp. 221–3, 392–6.

7. Rubin, op. cit., p. 175.

8. See Steedman, op. cit., pp. 110–31.

9. John Berger, *About Looking*, Writers and Readers, 1980, p. 101.

10. Paul Willis, 'Youth Unemployment: Ways of Living', *New Society*, 12 April 1984.

11. Steedman, op. cit., pp. 34–5, 125–9. Kathleen Woodward, *Jipping Street* (1928), Virago, 1983, Introduction.

12. Robert Roberts, *The Classic Slum*, Manchester University Press, Manchester, 1971, p. 160.

13. Richard Hoggart, *The Uses of Literacy* (1957), Penguin, 1959, p. 54.

14. For a brief account of John Pearman, see Carolyn Steedman, *Policing the Victorian Community*, Routledge & Kegan Paul, 1974, *passim*, and '*A Low Order of Men': John Pearman, Policeman*, Routledge & Kegan Paul (in press).

15. Dave Morley and Ken Worpole, *The Republic of Letters: Working Class Writing and Local Publishing*, Comedia, 1982, pp. 74–7.

16. ibid. See also David Vincent, *Bread, Knowledge and Freedom: A Study of Nineteenth Century Working Class Autobiography*, Methuen, 1981, pp. 8–9, 40, for the absence of women in working-class autobiography. Francis Place, *The Autobiography of Francis Place, 1771–1854*, ed. Mary Thane, Cambridge University Press, Cambridge, 1972, p. 21, for 'the best woman who ever lived'.

17. Woodward, op. cit., pp. 8–11, 15.

18. Kathleen Dayus, *Her People*, Virago, 1982. See below, pp. 93–5 for a discussion of this point.

19. Nancy Chodorow, *The Reproduction of Mothering: Psychoanalysis and the Sociology of Gender*, University of California Press, Berkeley and Los Angeles, 1978, p. 148.

20. Mitchell, op. cit., p. 380.

21. ibid., pp. 379–80. Mark Poster, *Critical Theory of the Family*, Seabury Press, New York, 1978, p. 198. Eli Zaretsky, *Capitalism, the Family and Personal Life*, Pluto, 1976. p. 61.

22. Michèle Barrett, *Women's Oppression Today*, Verso/NLB, 1980, pp. 202–4. Poster, op. cit., pp. 166–205.

23. E. P. Thompson, 'Happy Families', *New Society*, 8 September 1977.

24. Frederic Jameson, *The Political Unconscious*, Methuen, 1981, p. 156.

25. Juliet Mitchell, *Women: The Longest Revolution*, Virago, 1984, pp. 231–2.

26. Veronica Beechey, 'On Patriarchy', *Feminist Review*, 3 (1979) pp. 66–82.

27. Rubin, op. cit., pp. 165–9.

28. Mitchell, op. cit., p. 232.

29. ibid., p. 274.

30. Ann Oakley, *From Here to Maternity: Becoming a Mother*, Penguin, 1981, p. 10: 'Children are important, children are not important. Fertility is admired, barrenness commands respect. Women are put on this earth to have children; women are the breadwinners, and babies are a nuisance. Pregnancy means special treatment; pregnancy means work in a field or a factory, regardless . . . Motherhood is sacred; women are just people. A woman's achievement is twelve babies or twelve fields cared for . . .'. For an equally powerful description of the social meaning given to motherhood and the existence of children, see Ellen Moer's outline of Mary Shelley's myth of parturition in *Frankenstein*. Ellen Moers, *Literary Women*, The Women's Press, 1978, pp. 94–9.

31. Steedman, *The Tidy House*, pp. 19–25, pp. 111–13, pp. 146–7, pp. 150–51.

32. Quoted ibid., p. 97.

Reproduction and Refusal

1. Richard Hoggart, *The Uses of Literacy*, Penguin, 1959, p. 48.

2. Alice Schwarzer, *Simone de Beauvoir Today*, Chatto & Windus: The Hogarth Press, 1983, pp. 73–4, 76, 114–15.

3. When such behaviour is reported, it is seen as truly newsworthy: 'Four years ago my mother informed my sisters and myself that she had no desire to see us again. She gave no particular reason except to say that she "had had enough of families" . . . To our total astonishment three women admitted to similar experiences with their mothers . . .'. Christine Morris, 'What happens when a mother suddenly cuts the apron strings and closes her heart to her family?' *Guardian*, 21 August 1985.

4. Liz Stanley (ed.), *The Diaries of Hannah Cullwick*, Virago, 1984, p. 238.

5. ibid., p. 170.

6. ibid., p. 239.

7. Ann Oakley, *The Sociology of Housework*, Martin Robertson, 1974, pp. 165–80.

8. Carolyn Steedman, *The Tidy House: Little Girls Writing*, Virago, 1982, *passim*.

9. Sara Ruddick, 'Maternal Thinking', *Feminist Studies*, 6:2 (1980), pp. 341–67.

10. Nancy Chodorow, *The Reproduction of Mothering: Psychoanalysis and the Sociology of Gender*, University of California Press, Berkeley and Los Angeles, 1978.

11. ibid., pp. 108–10.

12. ibid., pp. 199–201.

13. ibid., p. 215.

14. ibid., p. 110.

15. Stanley, op. cit., pp. 49–50.

16. Judith Arcana, *Our Mothers' Daughters*, Shameless Hussy Press, Berkeley, California, 1979, pp. 171–2.

17. Adrienne Rich, *Of Woman Born*, Bantam, New York, 1977, p. 240.

18. ibid., p. 243.

19. Steedman, *The Tidy House*, pp. 119–28.

20. Evidence is drawn here from the Reports of the Children's Employment Commission (1862), PP 1863, xviii, p. 223; PP 1864, xxii, pp. 104–5, and *passim*. See also Eileen Yeo and E. P. Thompson, *The Unknown Mayhew*, Penguin, 1973, pp. 200, 213, for contemporary statements about the necessity of decent clothing for women and girls.

21. PP 1867, xviii, pp. 226–7.

22. Mark Poster, *Critical Theory of the Family*, Seabury Press, New York, 1978, pp. 172–3.

23. For a further exploration of the development of the sense of self through economic understanding, see Carolyn Steedman, '"Listen How the Caged Bird Sings": Amarjit's Song', in Carolyn Steedman, Cathy Urwin and Valerie Walkerdine (eds), *Language Gender and Childhood*, Routledge & Kegan Paul, 1986, pp. 137–63. See also Marion Glastonbury, 'The Best Kept Secret: How Working Class Women Live and What They Know', *Women's Studies International Quarterly*, 2 (1979), pp. 171–81.

24. Donald Winnicott, 'Communication Between Infant and Mother', in W. G. Joffe, (ed.) *What Is Psychoanalysis?*, Ballière, Tindall and Cassell, 1968, pp. 15–25, quoted in Madeleine Davis

and David Wallbridge, *Boundary and Space*, Penguin, 1981, p. 129.

25. ibid., p. 100.
26. Donald Winnicott, 'The Beginning of the Individual', 1966, unpublished paper, quoted in Davis and Wallbridge, op. cit., p. 100.
27. Jeremy Seabrook, *What Went Wrong?*, Gollancz, 1978, p. 122.
28. Kathleen Woodward, *Jipping Street* (1928), Virago, 1983, p. 18.
29. Rich, op. cit., p. 219.
30. Kathleen Dayus, *Her People*, Virago, 1982, p. 81.
31. Rich, op. cit., p. 219.
32. Stanley, op. cit., p. 168.
33. Woodward, op. cit., p. 20.
34. Rich, op. cit., pp. 248–9.
35. This is essentially the relationship described by Alice Miller in *The Drama of the Gifted Child*, Faber & Faber, 1983, though it is rather the drama of children who are made attentive and above all *good*, by a mother's need to find a solution to her own problems in a child. But see the next chapter.

Childhoods

1. Mary Wollstonecraft, *Mary: A Fiction* (1787), Schocken, New York, 1977, pp. 10–13.
2. Tamara Hareven, *Family Time and Industrial Time: The Relationship Between Family and Work in a New England Industrial Community*, Cambridge University Press, New York, 1982, p. 355.
3. Geoffrey Trodd, 'Political Change and the Working Class in Blackburn and Burnley, 1880–1914', Ph.D thesis, Lancaster, 1978, pp. 4, 13–14.
4. David Howell, *British Workers and the Independent Labour Party, 1886–1906*, Manchester University Press, Manchester, 1983, p. 56.
5. ibid., p. 55.
6. ibid.
7. Patrick Joyce, 'Popular Toryism in Lancashire, 1860–1890', Ph.D thesis, Oxford 1975, pp. 206–7. Jill Liddington and Jill Norris, *One Hand Tied Behind Us: The Rise of the Women's Suffrage Movement*, Virago, 1978, pp. 47–63.

8. ibid., p. 58.

9. Howell, op. cit., p. 56. See also Patrick Joyce, *Work, Society and Politics; The Culture of the Factory in Later Victorian England*, Harvester, Brighton, 1980, pp. 111–13.

10. Liddington and Norris, op. cit., pp. 47–63.

11. Jeremy Seabrook, *What Went Wrong?*, Gollancz, 1978, p. 139.

12. Jeremy Seabrook, *Working Class Childhood*, Gollancz, 1982, p. 139.

13. Seabrook, *What Went Wrong?*, p. 122.

14. Liddington and Norris, op. cit., pp. 95–6.

15. Trodd, op. cit., p. 15.

16. Hareven, op. cit., p. 361.

17. This was partly because she understood it to be a *political* definition, directly linked to a Labour perspective. See the next chapter for a fuller discussion of this point; and Part One, *Stories*.

18. Hareven, op. cit., p. 359.

19. ibid., pp. 359–60.

20. This check-list of good mothering is taken from Seabrook, *Working Class Childhood*, p. 139.

21. Liddington and Norris, op. cit., p. 57.

22. James Hinton, *Labour and Socialism: A History of the British Labour Movement, 1867–1974*, Wheatsheaf, Brighton, 1983, pp. 5–6.

23. Liddington and Norris, op. cit., p. 58.

24. Trodd, op. cit., pp. 36–7.

25. Alice Miller, *The Drama of the Gifted Child and the Search for the True Self*, Faber & Faber, 1983, pp. 44–5.

26. ibid., p. 29.

27. ibid., p. 29, 55.

28. ibid., p. 49.

29. ibid., pp. 49–50.

30. Robert Roberts, *The Classic Slum*, Manchester University Press, Manchester, 1971, pp. 21–2 for a potent source of description of these women.

31. See Part One, note 2.

32. Seabrook, *Working Class Childhood*, p. 147.

33. ibid., p. 202.

Exclusions

1. E. P. Thompson, *William Morris: Romantic to Revolutionary*, Pantheon, New York, 1976.
2. Wilhelm Reich, *What Is Class Consciousness?* (1934), Socialist Reproduction, n.d., pp. 40–4.
3. Melanie Klein, 'Love, Guilt and Reparation', in *Love, Guilt and Reparation and Other Works, 1921–1945*, Hogarth Press, 1975, pp. 306–7.
4. As Denise Riley points out in *War in the Nursery*, Virago, 1983, pp. 76–7.
5. Sigmund Freud, 'Family Romances' (1908), *Standard Edition of the Collected Works*, vol. 9, Hogarth Press, 1959, pp. 234–41; 'Some Character Types Met With in Psychoanalytic Work' (1916), *Standard Edition of the Collected Works*, vol. 14, 1957.
6. Richard Sennett and Jonathan Cobb, *The Hidden Injuries of Class*, Cambridge University Press, Cambridge, 1977.
7. Joseph T. Howell, *Hard Living on Clay Street*, Anchor/Doubleday, New York, 1973, pp. 1–8, 263–352.
8. Barbara Tizard and Martin Hughes, *Young Children Learning*, Fontana, 1984, pp. 73–132.
9. Robert McKenzie and Alan Silver, *Angels in Marble*, Heinemann, 1968, pp. 229–35.
10. ibid., pp. 190, 261. See also Pauline Hunt, *Gender and Class Consciousness*, Macmillan, 1980, pp. 171–9.
11. Jeremy Seabrook, *City Close-Up*, Penguin, 1973, p. 16.
12. 'The number of Labour activists owing their allegiance to the Conservative party was probably greater in Lancashire than anywhere else in the kingdom.' Patrick Joyce, *Work, Society and Politics: The Culture of the Factory in Later Victorian England*, Harvester, Brighton, 1980, p. 315.
13. Bob Jessop, *Conservatism and British Political Culture*, Allen & Unwin, 1974, pp. 144–94.
14. Elizabeth Gaskell, *North and South* (1855), Penguin, 1970, p. 110.
15. Geoffrey Trodd, 'Political Change and the Working Class in Blackburn and Burnley, 1880–1914', Ph.D. thesis, Lancaster, 1978, pp. 2, 5, 57.
16. ibid., pp. 44–62.
17. ibid., p. 2.
18. ibid., p. 44.

19. ibid., pp. 32, 44, 94, 98–103. Joyce, op. cit., pp. 256, 259.

20. Joyce, op. cit., p. 259.

21. ibid., p. 168.

22. Trodd, op. cit., p. 25.

23. Joyce, op. cit., pp. 198, 381.

24. Trodd, op. cit., p. 34.

25. Joyce, op. cit., pp. 111–13.

26. Jill Liddington and Jill Norris, *One Hand Tied Behind Us: The Rise of the Women's Suffrage Movement*, Virago, 1978, p. 95.

27. Louise A. Tilly and Joan W. Scott, *Women, Work and the Family*, Holt, Rinehart and Winston, Eastbourne, 1978, p. 212.

28. David Howell, *British Workers and the Independent Labour Party, 1886–1906*, Manchester University Press, Manchester, 1983, p. 58. Trodd, op. cit., pp. 13–14.

29. Gareth Stedman-Jones, 'Rethinking Chartism', in *Languages of Class*, Cambridge University Press, Cambridge, pp. 90–178.

30. ibid., p. 104.

31. ibid., pp. 101–2.

32. ibid.

33. Joyce, op. cit., pp. 313–14.

34. Howell, op. cit., pp. 52–68.

35. Joyce, op. cit., pp. 260, 313–15.

36. I do not mean to suggest that there isn't a female story of trade union organization, only that it is scarcely yet written. But see Sally Westwood, *All Day, Every Day*, Pluto, 1985.

37. McKensie and Silver, op. cit., pp. 187–90.

38. ibid., p. 261.

39. *Burnley Express*, 24 October 1908, quoted by Joyce, op. cit., pp. 277–8.

40. See above, pp. 27–47.

41. Gareth Stedman-Jones, 'Why Is the Labour Party in a Mess?', in Stedman-Jones, op. cit., p. 246.

Histories

1. William Labov, *Language in the Inner City*, University of Pennsylvania Press, Philadelphia, 1972, pp. 370–1.

2. Stephen Marcus, 'Freud and Dora: Story, History, Case-History', in *Representations: Essays on Literature and Society*, Macmillan, 1976, pp. 247–310.

3. Carolyn Steedman, *The Tidy House: Little Girls Writing*, Virago, 1982, pp. 61–84, 113–23.

4. William Thackeray, *Thackeray's Letters to An American Family*, introduced by Lucy W. Baxter, Smith, Elder, 1904, p. 32.

5. Hentry Mayhew, *London Labour and the London Poor* (4 vols), vol. 1, George Woodfall and Sons, 1851, pp. 151–2. The following extracts from the watercress-seller's narrative are all taken from this two-page transcript of 1851.

6. Sigmund Freud, 'Fragment of an Analysis of a Case of Hysteria ("Dora")' (1905), The Pelican Freud Library, vol. 8, *Case Histories 1*, Penguin, 1977, pp. 27–164.

7. For an example of the process of pathologizing through schooling, see Carolyn Steedman, ' "The Mother Made Conscious": The Historical Development of a Primary School Pedagogy', *History Workshop*, 20 (1985), pp. 149–63.

8. For a literary analysis of the romantic construction of childhood, see Peter Coveney, *Poor Monkey: The Child in Literature*, Rockliff, 1957, *passim*.

9. William Labov, *Language in the Inner City*, University of Pennsylvania Press, Philadelphia, 1972, pp. 390–3. In Labov's terms, the child was here orientating Mayhew, setting the scene for an eventual story. But the child does not go on to recount a particular event, as do the children and adolescents whose evidence is used in *Language in the Inner City*. In sociolinguistic terms, there is no label for the personal chronology – the autobiography – of the kind that the little watercress girl imparted.

10. Maria Ramas, 'Freud's Dora, Dora's Hysteria', in Judith L. Newton, Mary P. Ryan, Judith R. Walkowitz, (eds), *Sex and Class in Women's History*, Routledge & Kegan Paul, 1983, pp. 72–113.

11. Freud, 'Fragment of an Analysis', p. 66.

12. Ramas, op. cit., p. 73 and n. 5, pp. 107–8.

13. Freud, 'Fragment of an Analysis, p. 66.

14. Juliet Mitchell, *Women: The Longest Revolution: Essays in Feminism, Literature and Psychoanalysis*, Virago, 1984, p. 288.

15. Marcus, op. cit., pp. 276–8.

16. ibid., p. 278.

17. Freud, 'Fragment of an Analysis', pp. 56, 79.

18. ibid., p. 79.

19. ibid.

20. ibid., p. 163.

21. Sigmund Freud, 'From the History of an Infantile Neurosis (the "Wolf Man")' (1918), The Pelican Freud Library, vol. 9, *Case Histories II*, Penguin, 1979, pp. 287–90.

22. Lewis O. Mink, 'Everyman His or Her Own Annalist', *Critical Inquiry*, 7:4 (1981), pp. 777–83.

23. Freud, 'Fragment of an Analysis', p. 99.

24. ibid., pp. 104–5.

25. ibid., pp. 105–6.

26. Ramas, op. cit., pp. 88–90.

27. Freud 'Fragment of an Analysis', p. 47.

28. 'So in the "Dora" analysis, in which he unravels the tissues of sexual desire in an eighteen-year-old girl . . . Freud introduces the psychical complex that he is to reveal by the sort of sociological comment on families that would warm the heart of many a radical therapist today.' Juliet Mitchell, *Psychoanalysis and Feminism*, Penguin, 1975, pp. 63–4.

29. 'Perhaps you do not know that . . . "Schmuck-kastchen" is a favourite expression for the same thing that you alluded to not so long ago . . . for the female genitals, I mean.'

    'I knew that *you* would say that.'

    'That is to say, *you* knew that it *was* so.' (Freud, 'Fragment of an Analysis', p. 105.)

30. Labov, op. cit., pp. 366–70.

31. For a further discussion of nineteenth-century working-class children's understanding of economic selfhood, see Steedman, *The Tidy House*, pp. 110–31.

32. That is, she had paid 6d for them at the wholesale market.

33. The child remembered here her mother's earlier work: 'before I had the baby, I used to help mother, who was in the fur trade; and if there was any slits in the fur, I'd sew them up.'

34. Jonathan Culler, *The Pursuit of Signs*, Routledge & Kegan Paul, 1981, p. 201.

35. Jane Gallop, *Feminism and Psychoanalysis: The Daughter's Seduction*, Macmillan, 1982, pp. 141–50.

36. Ronald Fraser, *In Search of a Past*, Verso, 1984. History Workshop, 'In Search of an Author: A Dialogue with Ronald Fraser', *History Workshop Journal*, 20 (1985), pp. 175–88.

Childhood for a Good Woman

1. The Brothers Grimm, *Hansel and Gretel*, (illustrated by Anthony Browne), Julia MacRae, 1981. I had also recently read P. S. Rushforth, *Kindergarten*, Hamish Hamilton, 1979, which draws together the witch and the gingerbread house and recent historical horror.

2. Geoffrey Trodd, 'Political Change and the Working Class in Blackburn and Burnley, 1880–1914,' Ph.D, Lancaster, 1978, p. 24. Margaret Penn, *Manchester Fourteen Miles* (1947), Caliban, 1979, pp. 13–14.

3. William Harrison Ainsworth, *Lancashire Witches: A Novel* (1849), G. Routledge, 1884.

4. Trodd, op. cit., pp. 78–9 on the great liking of Lancashire workers for 'the herbalist and the quack doctor', and Patrick Joyce, 'Popular Toryism in Lancashire, 1860–1890', Ph.D, Oxford, 1975, on the possibility of Food Reform providing an entry to Independent Labour Party politics for some Lancashire workers in this period. See also Logie Barrow, 'Socialism in Eternity: The Ideology of Plebian Spiritualists, 1853–1913', *History Workshop Journal*, 9 (1980), pp. 37–69.

5. John Berger, *About Looking*, Writers & Readers, 1980, pp. 90–1, 94.

6. Jack Zipes, *Fairy Tales and the Art of Subversion*, Heinemann, 1983, pp. 77–96.

Bibliography

Ainsworth, William Harrison, *Lancashire Witches: A Novel* (1849), G. Routledge, 1884

Alexander, Sally, 'Women, Class and Sexual Difference', *History Workshop Journal*, 17 (1984), pp. 125–49

Andersen, Hans Christian, *Fairy Tales*, translated by H. L. Braekstad, with an introduction by Edmund Gosse (2 vols), Heinemann, 1900

Arcana, Judith, *Our Mothers' Daughters*, Shameless Hussy Press, Berkeley, California, 1979

Ashplant, Timothy, 'The New Social Function of Cinema', *Journal of the British Film Institute*, 79/80 (1981), pp. 107–9

Bamford, Samuel, *Early Days*, Simpkin & Marshall, 1849

Barrett, Michèle, *Women's Oppression Today*, Verso/NLB, 1980

Barrow, Logie, 'Socialism in Eternity: The Ideology of Plebian Spiritualists, 1853–1913', *History Workshop Journal*, 9 (1980), pp. 37–69

Beauvoir, Simone de, *A Very Easy Death* (1964), Penguin, 1969

Beechey, Veronica, 'On Patriarchy', *Feminist Review*, 3 (1979), pp. 66–82

Berger, John, *Ways of Seeing*, BBC/Penguin, 1972
    About Looking, Writers & Readers, 1980

Campbell, Beatrix, *Wigan Pier Revisited*, Virago, 1984

Chatman, Seymour, *Story and Discourse: Narrative Structure in Fiction and Film*, Cornell University Press, New York, 1978

Chodorow, Nancy, *The Reproduction of Mothering: Psychoanalysis and the Sociology of Gender*, University of California Press, Berkeley and Los Angeles, 1978

Cookson, Catherine, *Our Kate*, Macdonald, 1969

Coveney, Peter, *Poor Monkey: the Child in Literature*, Rockliff, 1957

Culler, Jonathan, *The Pursuit of Signs*, Routledge & Kegan Paul, 1981

Davis, Madeleine, and Wallbridge, David, *Boundary and Space*, Penguin, 1981

Dayus, Kathleen, *Her People*, Virago, 1982

Freud, Sigmund, 'Fragment of an Analysis of a Case of Hysteria ("Dora")', (1905) The Pelican Freud Library, vol. 8, *Case Histories I*, Penguin, 1977, pp. 27–164

'Family Romances' (1908), *Standard Edition of the Collected Works*, vol. 9, Hogarth Press, 1959, pp. 234–41

'Some Character Types Met With in Psychoanalytic Work' (1916), *Standard Edition of the Collected Works*, vol. 14, Hogarth Press, 1957

'From the History of an Infantile Neurosis (the "Wolf Man")' (1918), The Pelican Freud Library, vol. 9, *Case Histories II*, Penguin, 1979, pp. 287–90

Fraser, Ronald, *In Search of a Past*, Verso, 1984

Gallop, Jane, *Feminism and Psychoanalysis: The Daughter's Seduction*, Macmillan, 1982

Gaskell, Elizabeth Cleghorn, *North and South* (1855), Penguin, 1970

Glastonbury, Marion, 'The Best Kept Secret: How Working Class Women Live and What They Know', *Women's Studies International Quarterly*, 2 (1979), pp. 171–81

Grimm Brothers, *Hansel and Gretel* (illustrated by Anthony Browne), Julia MacRae, 1981

Hareven, Tamara, *Family Time and Industrial Time: The Relationship Between Family and Work in a New England Community*, Cambridge University Press, New York, 1982

Heron Liz (ed.), *Truth, Dare or Promise: Girls Growing Up in the 1950s*, Virago, 1985

Herriman, George, *Krazy Kat Komix*, vols 1–4, Real Free Press, Amsterdam, 1974–5

Hinton, James, *Labour and Socialism: A History of the British Labour Movement, 1867–1974*, Wheatsheaf, 1983

History Workshop, 'In Search of an Author: A Dialogue with Ronald Fraser', *History Workshop Journal*, 20 (1985), pp. 175–88

Hobsbawm, Eric, *Worlds of Labour*, Weidenfeld & Nicolson, 1984

Hoggart, Richard, *The Uses of Literacy*, Penguin, 1959

Howell, David, *British Workers and the Independent Labour Party, 1886–1906*, Manchester University Press, Manchester, 1983

Howell, Joseph T., *Hard Living on Clay Street*, Anchor/Doubleday, New York, 1973

Hunt, Pauline, *Gender and Class Consciousness*, Macmillan, 1980

Jameson, Frederic, *The Political Unconscious: Narrative as a Socially Symbolic Act*, Methuen, 1981

Jessop, Bob, *Conservatism and British Political Culture*, Allen & Unwin, 1974

Joyce, Patrick, 'Popular Toryism in Lancashire, 1860–1890', Ph.D. thesis, Oxford, 1975
  Work, Society and Politics: The Culture of the Factory in Later Victorian England, Harvester, Brighton, 1980

Kaplan, E. Ann, 'Is the Gaze Male?', in Ann Snitow *et al.* (eds), *Desire: The Politics of Female Sexuality*, Virago, 1984

Klein, Melanie, 'Love, Guilt and Reparation', in *Love, Guilt and Reparation and Other Works, 1921–1945*, Hogarth Press, 1975

Labov, William, *Language in the Inner City*, University of Pennsylvania Press, Philadelphia, 1972

Lewis, Jane, 'The Debate on Sex and Class', *New Left Review*, 149 (1985), pp. 108–20

Liddington, Jill, and Norris, Jill, *One Hand Tied Behind Us: The Rise of the Women's Suffrage Movement*, Virago, 1978

Lukas, George, *History and Class Consciousness*, Merlin Press, 1968

McKenzie, Robert, and Silver, Alan, *Angels in Marble*, Heinemann, 1968

Marcus, Steven, 'Freud and Dora: Story, History, Case-History', in *Representations: Essays on Literature and Society*, Random House, New York, 1976, pp. 247–310

Marx, Karl, 'Preface to "A Contribution to the Critique of Political Economy"' (1859), *Early Writings*, Pelican Marx Library, Penguin, 1975, pp. 424–8

Mayhew, Henry, *London Labour and the London Poor*, vol. 1, George Woodfall, 1851

Miller, Alice, *The Drama of the Gifted Child and the Search for the True Self*, Faber & Faber, 1983

Mink, Lewis O., 'Everyman His or Her Own Annalist', *Critical Inquiry*, 7:4 (1981), pp. 777–83

Mitchell, Juliet, *Psychoanalysis and Feminism*, Penguin, 1975
  Women: The Longest Revolution, Virago, 1984

Moers, Ellen, *Literary Women*, Women's Press, 1978

Morley, Dave, and Worpole, Ken, *The Republic of Letters: Working Class Writing and Local Publishing*, Comedia, 1982

Naipaul, V. S., *A House for Mr Biswas*, André Deutsch, 1961
  New York Review of Books, 24 November 1983

Newson, John and Elizabeth, *Seven Years Old in the Home Environment*, Allen & Unwin, 1976

Oakley, Ann, *The Sociology of Housework*, Martin Robertson, 1974

From Here to Maternity: Becoming a Mother, Penguin, 1981

Taking It Like a Woman, Cape, 1984

Owen, Ursula, (ed.), *Fathers: Reflections by Daughters*, Virago, 1983

Palmer, Roy, *A Touch on the Times: Songs of Social Change, 1770–1914*, Penguin, 1974

A Ballad History of England, Batsford, 1979

Penn, Margaret, *Manchester Fourteen Miles* (1947), Caliban, 1979

Pincus, Lily, and Dare, Christopher, *Secrets in the Family*, Faber & Faber, 1978

Place, Francis, *The Autobiography of Francis Place, 1771–1854*, (ed.) Mary, Thane, Cambridge University Press, Cambridge, 1972

Poster, Mark, *Critical Theory of the Family*, Seabury Press, New York, 1978

Ramas, Maria, 'Freud's Dora, Dora's Hysteria', in Judith L. Newton, Mary P. Ryan and Judith R. Walkowitz, (eds) *Sex and Class in Women's History*, Routledge & Kegan Paul, 1983, pp. 72–113

Reich, Wilhelm, *What Is Class Consciousness?* (1934), Socialist Reproduction, n.d.

Reports of the Children's Employment Commission (1862), PP 1863, xviii, PP 1864, xxii

Rich, Adrienne, *Of Woman Born*, Bantam, New York, 1977

Ricoeur, Paul, *Time and Narrative*, University of Chicago Press, Chicago, 1984

Riley, Denise, *War in the Nursery*, Virago, 1983

Roberts, Robert, *The Classic Slum*, Manchester University Press, Manchester, 1971

Rubin, Gayle, 'The Traffic in Women: Notes on the "Political Economy" of Sex', in Rayna R. Reiter, (ed.) *Towards an Anthropology of Women*, Monthly Reviews Press, New York, 1975

Ruddick, Sara, 'Maternal Thinking', *Feminist Studies*, 6:2 (1980) pp. 341–67

Schwarzer, Alice, *Simone de Beauvoir Today*, Chatto & Windus: The Hogarth Press, 1983

Seabrook, Jeremy, *City Close-Up*, Penguin, 1973

The Unprivileged (1967), Penguin, 1973

What Went Wrong?, Gollancz, 1978

Working Class Childhood, Gollancz, 1982

Sennett, Richard, and Cobb, Jonathan, *The Hidden Injuries of Class*, Cambridge University Press, Cambridge, 1977

Stanley, Liz, (ed.), *The Dairies of Hannah Cullwick*, Virago, 1984

Stedman-Jones, Gareth, *Languages of Class: Studies in English Work-*

ing Class History, 1832–1982, Cambridge University Press, Cambridge, 1983

Steedman, Carolyn, *The Tidy House: Little Girls Writing*, Virago, 1982

    Policing the Victorian Community, Routledge & Kegan Paul, 1984

    '"The Mother-Made-Conscious": The Historical Development of a Primary School Pedagogy', *History Workshop Journal*, 20 (1985), pp. 151–63

    'Listen How the Caged Bird Sings: Amarjit's Song', in Carolyn Steedman, Valerie Walkerdine and Cathy Urwin (eds), *Language, Gender and Childhood*, Routledge & Kegan Paul, 1985, pp. 137–63

Thackeray, W. M., *Thackeray's Letters to an American Family*, introduced by Lucy W. Baxter, Smith, Elder, 1904

Thompson, E. P., *The Making of the English Working Class*, Penguin, 1968

    William Morris: Romantic to Revolutionary, Pantheon, New York, 1976

    'Happy Families', *New Society*, 8 September 1977, pp. 499–501

Tilley, Louise A., and Scott, Joan W., *Women, Work and the Family*, Holt, Rinehart & Winston, 1978

Tizard, Barbara and Hughes, Martin, *Young Children Learning*, Fontana, 1984

Trodd, Geoffrey, 'Political Change and the Working Class in Blackburn and Burnley, 1880–1914', Ph.D, Lancaster, 1978

Vincent, David, *Bread, Knowledge and Freedom: A Study of Nineteenth Century Working Class Autobiography*, Methuen, 1981

Westwood, Sally, *All Day, Every Day*, Pluto, 1985

White, Hayden, 'The Value of Narrativity in the Representation of Reality', *Critical Inquiry*, 7:1 (1980), pp. 5–27

Williams, Raymond, *Politics and Letters*, NLB/Verso, 1979

Willis, Paul, 'Youth Unemployment: Ways of Living', *New Society*, 12 April 1984

Winnicott, Donald, 'The Beginning of the Individual', 1966 (unpublished paper)

    'Communication Between Infant and Mother', in W. G. Joffé, *What Is Psychoanalysis?*, Ballière, Tindall and Cassell, 1968, pp. 15–25

    Playing and Reality, Penguin, 1974

Winstanley, Gerrard, 'The Law of Freedom in a Platform; or True Magistracy Restored' (1652), in George H. Sabine (ed.), *The Works of Gerrard Winstanley*, Cornell University Press, New York, 1941

Woodward, Kathleen, *Jipping Street* (1928), Virago, 1983

Yeo, Eileen, and Thompson, E. P., *The Unknown Mayhew*, Penguin, 1973

Young, Michael, and Willmott, Peter, *Family and Kinship in East London*, Penguin, 1962

Zaretsky, Eli, *Capitalism, the Family and Personal Life*, Pluto, 1976

Zipes, Jack, *Fairy Tales and the Act of Subversion*, Heinemann, 1983

Index